7 DIMENSIONS OF SINGING
THE THROGA® TECHNIQUE

BY RICHARD FINK IV

7 Dimensions of Singing

Edited by Andrew Phan

Anatomy illustrations by Rebecca King (Renegade Chihuahua)
Book design and chapter illustrations by Richard Fink IV
Cover by Lyndsay Polizzi

© 2016-23 Richard Fink IV
All rights reserved. No part of this publication may be reproduced, stored in a retrieval system, or transmitted in any form or by any means; electronic, mechanical, photocopy, recording, or otherwise, without the written permission of the copyright owner.

Printed in the United States
Second Edition

Published by Throga LLC
PO Box 562
Bergen, NY 14416 USA

www.THROGA.com

ISBN: 978-1-7328869-0-2

To my students; past, present, and future:
You are collectively my greatest teacher. I am both humbled and honored to have experienced your voices in their most vulnerable states. I hope each and every one of you continues to develop and share your incredible instrument for the world to hear.

Acknowledgments

Thank you;

Alysia, Ada, and Aurora for believing in me and continuing to endure countless late nights and early mornings of my working to pursue my passion; **Andrew Phan** for your guidance, insight, and unrelenting honesty, in which this book would not have been possible otherwise; **Mark Baxter** for continuously inspiring me to become the best teacher I can be and for always encouraging me to sing through both the good and the bad; My parents, **Susan** and **Richard**, for setting the bar high enough to teach me the value in fighting for what I believe in; **Johnny Cummings** for helping me to forge a career in music and singing over the past 25 years of collaborating in countless projects; **Sam Polizzi** for always being there to lend your audio expertise; **Jason Reid** for your faith in me and guidance in the world of business; **Kathy White** and **Barb Galiford** for making me feel like a singer long before anyone else took notice and for planting the seeds of joy in teaching others; **Tony Gross** for helping me navigate the music industry during my early years; **George Collichio** for giving an eager young man his first shot at teaching; **Theodis Anderson** for believing in my voice and creating opportunities at a time when no one else would; **Certified Throga Instructors** for beating Throga's proverbial drum in an effort to help others reveal their gift as singers; **Gretchen Roth** for your continuous support; **Jim Bostock** for your contributed knowledge while writing this book; **Kemo Bunguric & JMC Academy** for welcoming the Throga technique into a new community of singers; **Sarah Thiele** for your encouragement and inspiration during Throga's early developmental stages; and finally, **Ted Neeley**, for illuminating a path to inspire and bring hope to others through singing, storytelling, and above all, compassion.

Foreword

Are you curious? That's great! Because an inquisitive mind is a wonderful way to approach the brilliance of the "7 Dimensions of Singing." It's my honor to introduce its creator, Richard Fink IV. It's fitting to note that it was *his curiosity* that gave birth to this unique concept. But it's also fitting to note that his curiosity did not rest until every dimension of the voice was integrated like never before. Curiosity leads to possibilities. Commitment leads to success.

I met Richard many years ago as a student in my Manhattan studio. He may be a three-time Guinness World Record holder for certain vocal abilities, but he also owns the record in my book for the most questions asked during a singing lesson! It was during those early sessions that Richard quickly established himself as a vocal scholar. Years later, not only did I give him my blessing to become a teacher, but I was excited for his future students. Many singers teach at some point; few are as passionate about vocal physiology and the physics of sound as Richard.

Even now, Richard continues to challenge the status quo of vocal improvement. Acceptance leads to complacency. The culmination of this relentless pursuit to incorporate every aspect of singing into one system resulted in something never achieved by any vocal pedagogue in history: a U.S. patent. As impressive as this achievement is, what makes Richard a special teacher is not something that was acquired from years of study and hard work. It's his compassion.

You can't teach someone to care. It is Richard's compassion for helping others that sparks his curiosity and fuels his drive. It's beautiful. Compassion leads to connection. It's why I am excited for you as you embark on this multi-dimensional journey of self-improvement. Yes, this program is about singing but there is nothing more reflective of the soul than your voice. Everything you need to transform the singer within is here. And should you run a little low on motivation, you've got Richard Fink IV as inspiration. Be curious. Be committed. Be compassionate. Singing leads to love.

- **Mark Baxter**
  World-Renowned Vocal Authority

Contents

Introduction 1
How Your Instrument Works 5
What Is Throga? 11
    Vocal Gym 14
    Throga Guidelines 15
    7 Dimensions of Singing 19
Flexibility: 1st Dimension 23
    Flexibility Exercise 28
Breathing: 2nd Dimension 33
    Breathing Exercise 39
Intonation: 3rd Dimension 43
    Intonation Exercise 48
Range: 4th Dimension 53
    Range Exercise 60
Tone: 5th Dimension 65
    Tone Exercise 72
Articulation: 6th Dimension 77
    Articulation Exercise 83
Strength: 7th Dimension 87
    Strength Exercise 91
7DS on Stage 97
    Mindful Singing 99

7 Dimensions of Singing

Diagnostics and Solutions 107
   On and Off Stage Solutions 110
      Flexibility Solutions 112
      Breathing Solutions 113
      Intonation Solutions 114
      Range Solutions 115
      Tone Solutions 117
      Articulation Solutions 118
      Strength Solutions 119
   Mistakes On Stage 121
Vocal Exercise Mapping 125
   Formant 130
   Feature 131
   Pattern 132
   Volume 133
   Tempo 134
   Variable 135
It's the Journal, Not the Destination 145
   Vocal Gym Journal 148
   How Often Should I Practice? 152
   How Do I Know If I'm Improving? 153
Glossary of Terms 159
About the Author 171

Introduction

"If you can speak, you can sing."

This statement stirs a fair amount of controversy among those who believe one must be "born to sing" in order to sing well. However, we're all generally born equal in our abilities to do so. Imagine, for a second, a doctor looking inside your throat through an X-ray machine. Without ever hearing your voice, would it be possible for her, or any other type of specialist, to know if you speak with a southern accent, can sing in tune, or have a "whiney" tone of voice, or even if you could reach high notes when singing?

No.

These are all behavioral traits, not genetic predispositions. The sound of your voice is only partially due to its shape and size (your genetics), and how it is cared for (your general health). Most of the sound comes from how you play it.

If that's true, you may be wondering why there's so much variation as we age, or why some appear to have a more "natural" ability to sing than others. The reason for this is that singing has little to do with our DNA and a whole lot to do with how we coordinate and program ourselves to sound, particularly during the first seven years of childhood.

We spend those formative years mimicking the tone, volume, delivery, and dialect of our parents' voices when learning to speak and the voices singing in our home, on the radio, and at church. Our social and environmental surroundings all play a role in the development of our voice. This is why there can be thousands of different people singing the same song, with thousands of different results.

So what does that all mean? It means that with the right training, you can dramatically change the actions of your instrument and therefore, the sound of your voice. The first step to making this happen is to acknowledge that CHANGE IS POSSIBLE.

"Our beliefs control our bodies, our minds and thus our lives..."

- Bruce H. Lipton (1944 -)

Our voices are a reflection of our beliefs, personality, life experience, and desires. For some of us, those life experiences and desires pushed us to study and practice often, to meet or exceed the public standard of what is generally accepted as being a "good" singer. But what's wrong with singing purely for the love of singing?

Absolutely nothing.

In most modern societies, singing for the purpose of self-expression, communication, and human connection has become greatly diluted. Its purity slowly evolved into a regimented and competitive art form over the past several hundred years. This shift morphed singing into a means of reverence, social acceptance, and monetization as a highly profitable machine. Naturally, everyone should be encouraged to pursue a higher degree of vocal skill for a multitude of reasons, but it is essential that we don't lose sight of why we sing in the first place.

The goal of this book is to challenge your perspectives and share insights into the vocal instrument that will lead you to reach your goals, just as my teachers, students, and studies have done for me. Throughout my journey so far, I've been very fortunate to work with many culturally and stylistically diverse singers, speakers, and educators. They have entrusted me with a lifetime of inspirational, fun, tragic, and overall healing stories that have shown me the true value of singing and its ability to cultivate the inner self. These stories, a few of which I will be sharing with you, are all connected as the inspiration to the *7 Dimensions of Singing: The Throga Technique*.

Whether you're just starting out or a seasoned professional, I urge you to be vulnerable. What separates Throga from other techniques isn't the exercises suggested within this book, but rather the understanding of *which* exercises you should focus on and *how* they should be practiced. Learn from your mistakes and be open to change, as we take this journey on improving not just our voices, but ourselves, in the process.

> ***7DS Book Media**: Additional downloadable materials, including audio and journal templates referenced in this book, are available at throga.com.*

The Throga Technique

How Your Instrument Works

Chapter I

Before we dive into Throga, we should first familiarize ourselves with the basics of how our instrument works. Up until the last quarter of the 20th century, those who were interested in developing and refining their vocal abilities used techniques derived from mimicry, observational science, and speculation. Lucky for us, with today's technological advances, such as the use of fiber optic and video laryngoscopes, spirometers, spectrometers, MRI, fMRI, and CAT scan machines, we no longer need to guess.

Like any other musical instrument, the voice requires four fundamental elements to produce a controlled sound: First, is the means to convert energy into motion, this is known as an "actuator" (your breath). Next, is a surface to react to that motion, known as a "vibrator" (your vocal folds). The pressure waves from the vibration then bounce around a chamber, expanding the sound, this is known as a "resonator" (your vocal tract). The final element is to help refine and shape the sound, known as an "articulator" (your tongue, jaw, and lips). However, unlike other musical instruments, the musician is neurologically attached to the instrument itself. Therefore, the brain must first initiate the intent to vocalize by instructing the body to inhale.

The inhalation process involves the diaphragm (a large dome-shaped muscle underneath the lungs that separates the chest from the abdomen) and external intercostal muscles (woven between the ribs of your rib cage), which flex to expand the lungs and draw air inward. All of this is regulated by the brain and the vocalist's intention throughout the vocalizing process.

In the following diagram, we can see the cycle of events that takes place whenever we phonate, which means to speak or sing:

The Throga Technique

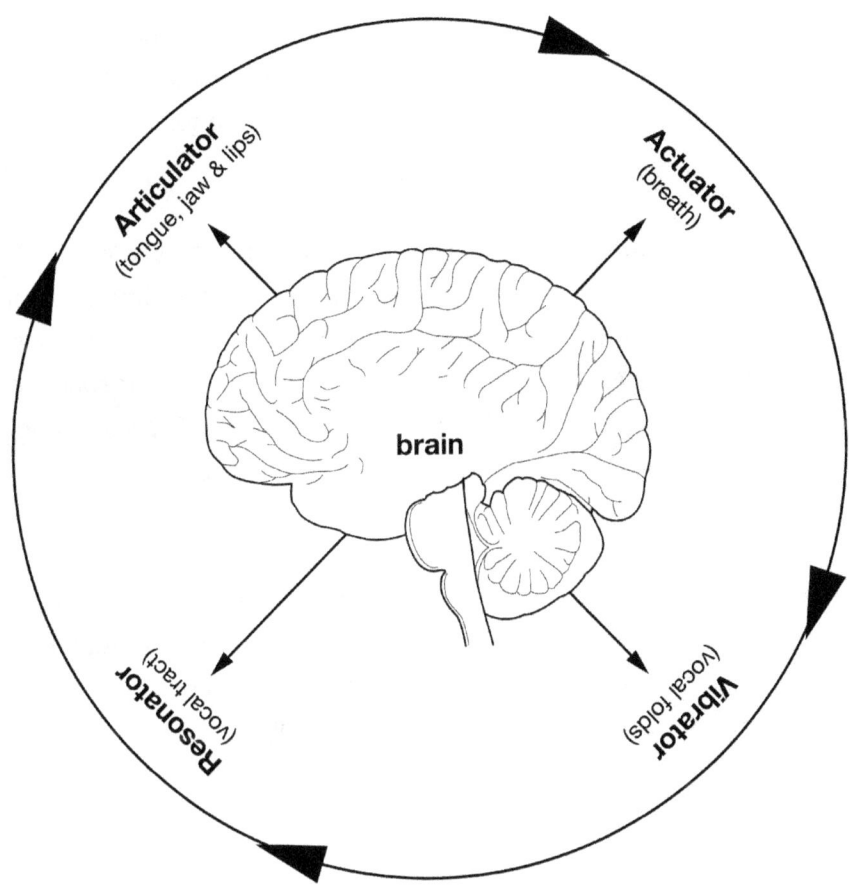

(1) **Actuation:** Air is released through a controlled relaxation of the inhalation muscles working against the abdominals and internal intercostal muscles of the rib cage. The released air pressure (our breath) acts as the instrument's actuator. It sends air upwards from the lungs and through the larynx (our voice box), which is at the top of the trachea, just under the U-shaped bone called the hyoid.

(2) **Vibration:** The vocal folds, housed inside of your larynx, then come together against the released air, causing them to

vibrate via the Bernoulli Effect (a principle of physics that causes a cycle of vibration) at various speeds in response to the tension of the folds. The vibration of the folds is formally known as a mucosal wave.

(3) **Resonation:** The movement of the vocal folds pushes air molecules around, creating a sound wave (the fundamental frequency). This adjustable wave is then enhanced and molded into desired tones in response to the resonating chambers of space known as the vocal tract. The vocal tract includes the pharynx (your throat), oral cavities, and nasal cavities.

(4) **Articulation:** The enhanced frequency can then be fine-tuned and intentionally disrupted to create identifiable shapes and sounds (our vowels and consonants) by adjusting the muscles related to the tongue, the jaw, and the lips.

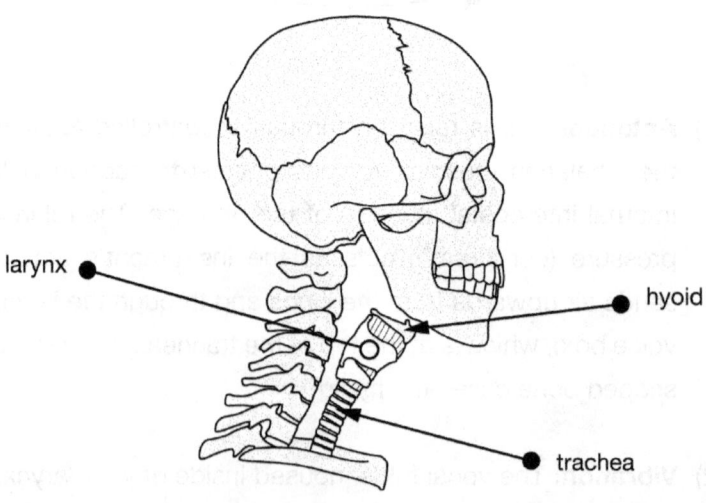

That was a lot of technical jargon! With that aside, it's important to note the meaning of many keywords and phrases used throughout this book should be based in context. Our previous experiences with a word or concept in a new setting can sometimes be misleading. This is especially true in the field of vocal technique, where many seemingly similar disciplines, beliefs, and antiquated phrasings are highly controversial.

If at any point you feel something might be contradictive to your current knowledge or studies, take a moment to refer to the *Glossary of Terms* towards the back of the book. Don't worry; you don't need to memorize it to sing at your best!

How Your Instrument Works Summary

- Singing starts in the mind.

- The vocal instrument is made up of four parts: actuator (breath), vibrator (vocal folds), resonator (vocal tract), and articulators (tongue, jaw, and lips).

- Don't let the technical jargon used in this book intimidate you in your ability to benefit from it.

What Is Throga?
Chapter II

Many years ago, a singer-songwriter by the name of Sarah was struggling to maintain a consistent voice during her nightly performances at a casino in Las Vegas. Allergies, stress, and recovering from having recently quit smoking, resulting in an overly sensitive and unreliable instrument. It was in this setting that the term "throga" was born. Sarah needed to practice mindful vocalizing, casually referred to as "yoga for the throat," in order to gain a better balance of mental and physical behaviors.

From a scientific perspective, both yoga and vocalizing create resonant postures designed to maximize energy with minimal efforts, consciously connecting the mind (the singer) and the body (the instrument). Throga's philosophy is to celebrate one's unique vocal qualities while striving to build a healthy, strong, and well-balanced instrument for self-expression. It is through this lens that Sarah, and other singers around the world, have been able to reach their goals.

Throga's tools, or techniques, were created to take advantage of how the neural pathways in our brain work for mental programming (skill building); primarily consisting of two concepts:

(1) The *Throga Guidelines*: Rules to follow when exploring vocal exercises in the "vocal gym." They are designed to increase awareness and developmental efficiency.

(2) The *7 Dimensions of Singing*: A systematic approach based on vocal physiology that accurately targets any aspect of your voice during vocal training.

These tools will help break down the complexities and mysteries of your voice, while providing a logical approach to developing it, regardless of your experience, age, vocal style, or skill. The reason it works universally is that Throga's focus is on the vocalist's fundamental behaviors, rather than the style or identifiable traits featured within a genre. For example, classical singers use a targeted speed of vibrato, shaping the vowels, and specific overtones. Pop singers use conversational qualities such as the use of "vocal fry", breathy tones, or "glottal shocks." Metal singers use a strategic force of air pressure and placement of tension to disrupt and distort selected pitches.

At the core of these genres can be the same instrument played with different intentions. A skilled violinist, for instance, can use the same finely crafted violin to play a part of a string quartet in a German opera house, or as part of a honkytonk band in a New Orleans's bar. Certainly, the traits relative to each style may require additional guidance or technique, but the better the foundation, the easier it is to build upon.

The training used to build a strong vocal foundation usually involves a variety of exercises, many of which are shared or similar in nature among teachers of all methodologies. The same can be said for personal trainers who recommend similar, if not identical, fitness exercises. They might ask their clients to do an "ab" exercise to improve core strength, but what kind should YOU do? How often? How many? How fast? And in what sequence with other exercises should that be done?

Knowing the answers to these types of questions, based on your history, current abilities, and goals, will no doubt accelerate your progress. Once you're familiar with Throga's tools, you can essentially become your own personal trainer. But every trainer requires a space to exercise and expand his or her knowledge, which brings us to our next topic, the vocal gym.

Vocal Gym

When a basketball player goes to a gym to work out, he isn't concerned about how much time is left on the shot clock (in fact, there isn't even a shot clock), whom to pass the ball to, where his opponent is, or how much winning the game will affect his career (there is no game). Instead, he's focused on targeting specific muscle groups in his body to gain coordination, strength, and agility, which will allow him to respond with more precision and stamina on the court. The same can be accomplished for vocalists by focusing on targeted muscle groups in the vocal gym so that they can respond with more precision and stamina in the moment, or on the stage.

The good news is, you were born with a free lifetime-membership and 24-hour access to your very own personalized vocal gym. The bad news is, no one has ever progressed by just owning a gym membership. You have to put in the time and effort to use the equipment inside. Proper training and awareness (good form) are what allows a runner to run, a dancer to dance, and a singer to sing at his or her best.

To create a well-balanced voice, you need to develop a wide variety of tonal expressions, skills, dynamics, and freedom throughout your vocal range. To work on this, vulnerability is essential so that you feel unencumbered during the training process. A quiet, private space makes it easier to let your guard down. That way, there's no temptation to force an exercise to sound "better" if you think someone else might be able to hear you. If this type of environment is hard for you to come by, remember that your voice is ALWAYS with you. The old adage, "Where there is a will, there is a way," can easily be applied here.

Vocalizing can be done in countless scenarios throughout the day. Whether you're out walking your dog, in the restroom, riding an elevator, relaxing on the couch, making breakfast, in a deserted aisle at the grocery store, filling the car with gas, waking up in the shower, shuffling through the school hallways, or on your way to work by car, bus, subway, train, airplane... you get the idea!

The point is, you can make time to reach your goals regardless of lifestyle and general activities. Even if you only work in a few minutes here and there, they can add up fast and truly make a difference in the long run. The more quality time you spend in the vocal gym, the better, but don't rush the process. Like any other physical training, if you race through your warmups or push too hard, it can lead to fatigue. It will reinforce negative behaviors and slow development.

When vocalizing, you're not aiming to test the tensile strength of your voice. The muscles of the larynx are very small and sensitive, yet very durable and reliable when managed correctly. The physical capacity and endurance of your voice will come with proper training over time.

SO DON'T RUSH.

In a later chapter, *It's the Journal, Not the Destination*, we'll discuss how to create a customizable vocal routine to maximize your progress. With the vocal gym setup, we can now introduce the *Throga Guidelines* and the *7 Dimensions of Singing*.

Throga Guidelines

All gyms and training techniques have rules to follow and for good reason. As singers, we often modify an exercise in order to sound as good as possible, as fast as possible. This would be like trying to lift heavy weights before properly addressing the related muscles and coordination to do so. Unfortunately, this "quick-fix" approach to reaching a goal requires sacrificing good form and tends to misdirect the mental and physical programming we need to continually improve. It ignores signs of imbalance, tension, or even discomfort at times and will inevitably lead to inconsistent performances and results.

The *Throga Guidelines* cultivate awareness and assist in the isolation of only the necessary muscle groups within a given exercise. This allows for a much healthier and more efficient training experience. While exploring the exercises in the upcoming chapters, be sure to come back to review the guidelines. For some exercises, you may find it relatively easy to juggle them all at once. For others, it might take days, weeks, or even months to apply the guidelines effortlessly. This doesn't mean you're doing anything wrong. In fact, just the opposite is true.

Acquiring the ability to identify vocal imbalances within your practice means that you've honed in on key factors that are holding you back from your true potential. This is great news because now you'll know what to focus on to reach your goals. The sooner you reveal and acknowledge these imbalances, no matter how poorly an exercise may sound at first, the sooner you will start to notice positive changes within your voice when singing.

"Learn the rules like a pro, so you can break them like an artist."

- Pablo Picasso (1881 - 1973)

The following guidelines can be applied to any vocal exercise, but only in the mindset of the vocal gym:

Maintain Tempo: The tempo(s) or duration intended at the start of an exercise should remain constant throughout the exercise.

This guideline will not only help you improve your overall sense of timing when you sing, it will also improve your breath control by denying the temptation to speed up. We often due to overspending air at the beginning of a phrase.

Maintain Volume: The volume(s) intended at the start of an exercise should remain consistent throughout the exercise.

When singing, the volume is often inadvertently raised to secure a higher pitch. This guideline will help you develop valuable independence between pitch and volume, which will positively impact your ability to dynamically express yourself within a song.

Maintain Formant: A formant, or a sustained sound such as an ē, ä, m, or a lip-trill (discussed in a later chapter) should only be modified if it is a deliberate intention within an exercise.

Similar to volume, formants are sometimes unintentionally modified in order to make it easier to sing pitches or tones. This can rob you of your vocal freedom when singing and distract listeners if they struggle to understand the poetry being presented.

Maintain a Clear Tone: Avoid any breathy or distorted vocal sounds unless it is a deliberate focus within the exercise (such as adding a "vocal fry").

An airy or distorted sound generally indicates an imbalance of air pressure or excess tension. It can also be a sign of vocal fatigue, inflammation of the folds, or some other pathology. Depending on the genre, imbalanced textures may be welcomed into the performance of a song, but it's best not to stylize an exercise with a sound that may mask your voice's true condition.

No Exterior Muscles: Avoid any unintentional facial movements or visible signs of tension in the neck or shoulder area.

Learning to control your voice, without unnecessary muscles jumping in to help with the control of pitch or breathing, will lead to more freedom in tonal expression. This guideline will also assist in avoiding awkward or unwanted facial expressions when singing.

Minimize Vibrato: Avoid adding vibrato unless it is a deliberate focus within an exercise.

Vibrato can be a wonderful asset in the delivery of a song, but when vocalizing, it can mask imbalances we are hoping to discover and improve upon. It's okay if a little shows up here and there, particularly toward the end of an exercise. However, make a conscious effort not to perform the exercise with vibrato in an attempt to make it sound "better." Remember, the more raw a sound is, the more honest it will be to work with.

Let Go: Maintaining a tension-free environment takes precedence over forcing notes within an exercise.

Letting go of a note, no matter how bad it may sound, will allow you to temporarily expose a lack of coordination. Unlike singing a song, maintaining good form in the vocal gym is more important than sounding good. So if a note occasionally disappears, cracks, skips, or jumps while doing an exercise, don't stress.

7 Dimensions of Singing

The *7 Dimensions of Singing* identifies each dimension of the voice, and more importantly, it helps us to target them with the right exercises. Vocalizing, the act of creating intentional vocal sounds and behaviors, requires an incredible network of nerves, muscles, living tissue, and intricate moving parts. Knowing which exercises to spend your time on is essential to creating balance and discovering your true vocal potential. Though they may not all be equal within a given exercise or performance, there isn't any *one* dimension more or less valuable than the others. They are:

1. **Flexibility**: The pliability of the vocal folds

2. **Breathing**: The control of our beath

3. **Intonation**: The control of our pitch

4. **Range**: The vocal balance from the lowest to highest note

5. **Tone**: The quality of sound

6. **Articulation**: How we pronounce words

7. **Strength**: The stability and stamina of the voice

Since the muscles in our body never act alone, the ones referenced to describe the actions of each dimension are dominant, but they're not exclusive. For example, the bicep in your arm can be used to lift and hold a gallon of water, but they require a myriad of other muscles acting in an opposing relationship to stabilize the arm and the body's posture in the process. In the same way that you can isolate areas of your body when working out, such as curling barbells to target the biceps, vocal exercises will target specific areas of your voice.

What is Throga? Summary

- The term Throga originated from throat-yoga.

- Throga techniques are safe to apply to any age, singing style and skill level.

- Throga is designed to build a singer's foundation and to improve vocal behaviors, not the style of delivery.

- The vocal gym is a state of mind that can be accessed at any time (a quiet place away from anyone is best).

- The *Throga Guidelines* assist with form when training, which takes precedence over the pleasantness of sound.

- The *7 Dimensions of Singing* will allow you to dissect your voice and target what you need to improve in an exercise.

- Balancing your voice is key to singing the way you want.

- There are no shortcuts to REAL change.

Flexibility: 1st Dimension

Chapter III

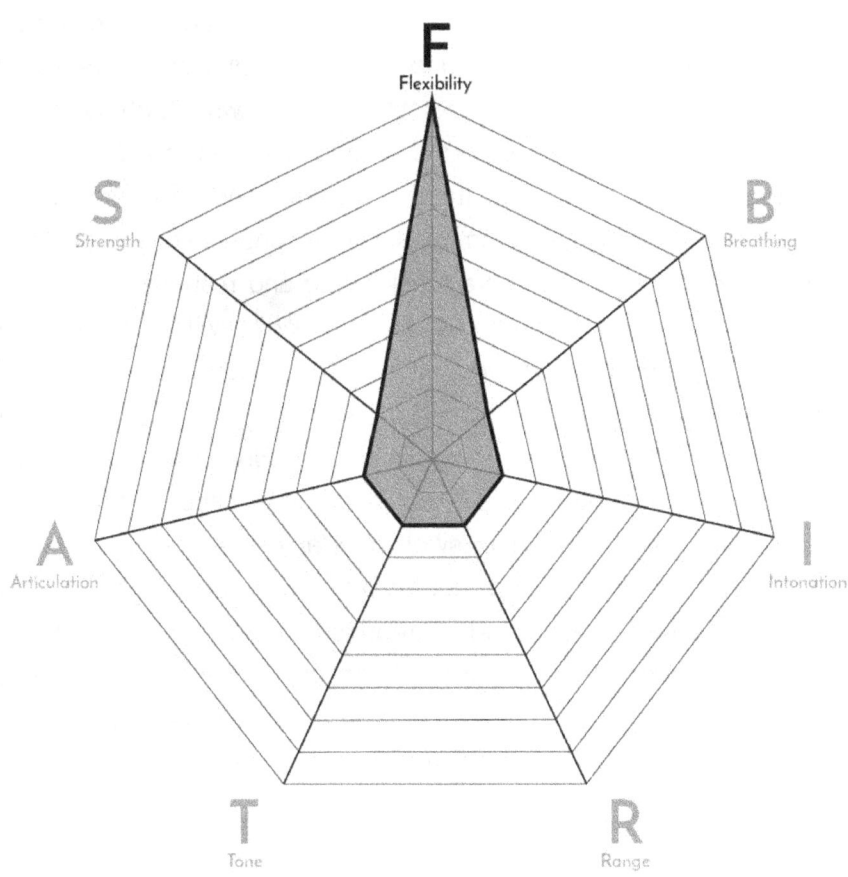

Flexibility: The pliability of the vocal folds

Have you ever tried to run as fast as you possibly can? Or perhaps as far as you can? If so, you probably discovered pretty quickly how valuable stretching your legs can be beforehand. Not to mention how much your muscles may beg you to stretch and massage them afterward.

Loosening up before any physical activity such as running, cycling, or swimming, makes you feel better and almost always leads to better results. Singing is no exception. This is why *flexibility* is the first of the seven dimensions and ideal to start with in your warmups.

When you sing, muscles throughout your body are needed to execute your musical and emotional intentions from one fleeting moment to the next. The more tension-free and responsive they all are, the better. However, when we refer to *flexibility* within the context of the *7 Dimensions of Singing*, we're talking specifically about the pliability of the vocal folds.

The vocal folds, as you may recall from *How Your Instrument Works*, are what vibrate to create sound when you speak and sing. If the folds are tight, stressed, or swollen for any reason, your ability to generate a consistent and controlled sound becomes limited. Particularly on higher notes, which require them to vibrate at a faster speed than lower notes. The overall elasticity of the vocal folds are based on the disengagement of the thyroarytenoid muscles located inside your larynx, along with the agility of all five vocal fold layers.

> *NOTE: Consuming enough water is crucial to maintaining a healthy voice. Being well-hydrated will keep your vocal folds lubricated, which helps to reduce friction and fatigue.*

The Throga Technique

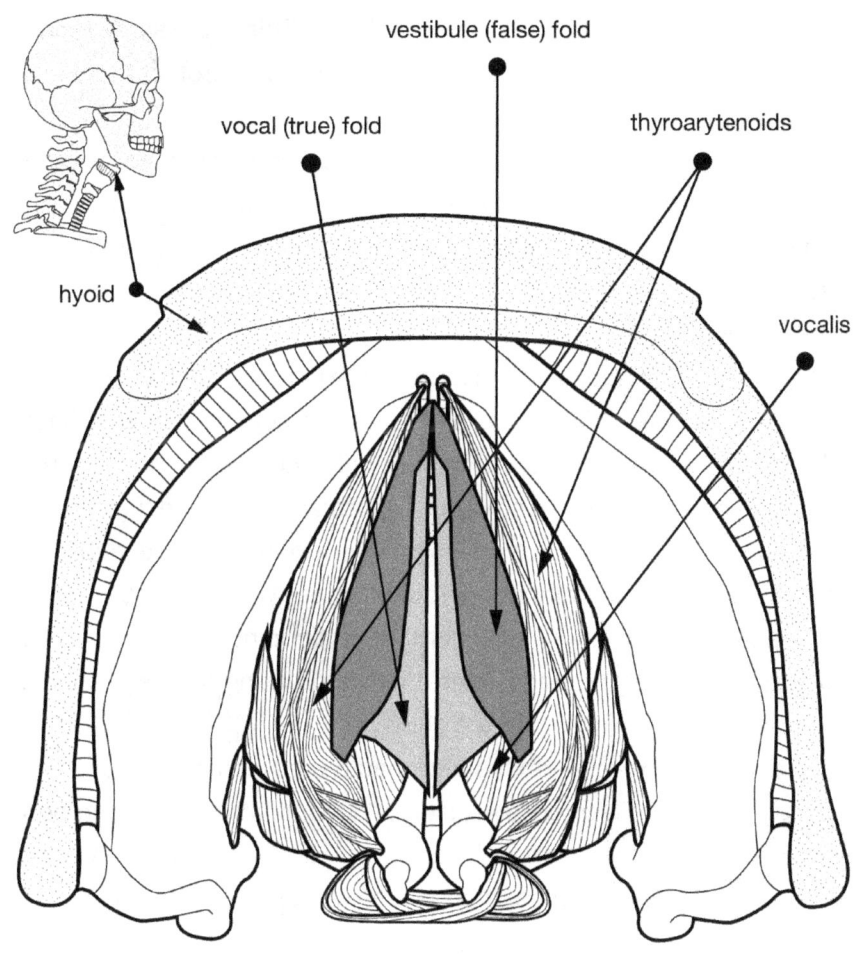

* top view of larynx

The innermost layer of the vocal folds is an extension of the thyroarytenoid muscle known as the vocalis, which helps stiffen and position the vocal folds' length and mass. The middle three vibrating layers are deep, intermediate, and superficial. These are collectively known as the lamina propria or LP for short. The LP layers have a high liking to water in the form of hyaluronic acid, which is needed to vibrate and create sound freely. The fifth and outermost layer of the

7 Dimensions of Singing

folds, the epithelium, is only a few cells thick. This is the same type of surface as the inside of your cheek, which helps to protect them from abrasion.

Incidentally, the larynx also consists of a second set of folds called the vestibular folds. These "false" folds are situated just above the "true" vocal folds and can aid in the creation of tonal textures, often used in rock and aggressive styles of singing, though it's not their primary function.

Several years ago, a young man by the name of Jack was leading up to a milestone performance in his career: a sold-out show at Radio City Music Hall in New York City. Not only was it a full house, but it was also the fastest selling sold-out performance in the venue's famed eighty-plus-year history. The record label executives and publicists were all in attendance, along with radio contest-winners, close friends, and family members. All of whom were flooding the dark narrow hallways between the stage door and the dressing rooms waiting in line to speak with him before the show.

Despite the basic warmups Jack had done when he first woke up, the early morning TV interviews, lack of accumulative sleep, and non-stop talking over the course of the day had taken its toll on his voice. Now, just forty-five minutes to showtime, it was obvious from just his speaking voice that Jack's vocal folds were swollen from friction and fatigue. The unusually airy quality with occasional dropouts of sound when he spoke, gave it all away all easily. Since an extended period of vocal rest wasn't an option, what could Jack have done?

Depending on the circumstances, you may find that you only need to warmup for a few minutes to get the responsiveness you're looking for. Other times, you may have to focus on *flexibility* exercises throughout the day. This is especially true if you're wrestling with a head cold or allergies, or maybe recovering from a late night talking over loud music, or even cheering on your favorite team. And of course, if you're a traveling professional having to constantly adapt to rapidly changing environments, such as our friend Jack, nervously waiting backstage in his makeshift "Radio City Vocal Gym."

In Jack's scenario, it's a good idea to do vocal exercises that have a rejuvenating quality prior to jumping into a normal warmup routine. The objective is to allow the folds to vibrate with more freedom, which we can do by focusing on the dimension of *flexibility*.

Flexibility Exercise
("Mē" descending glissando into vocal fry)

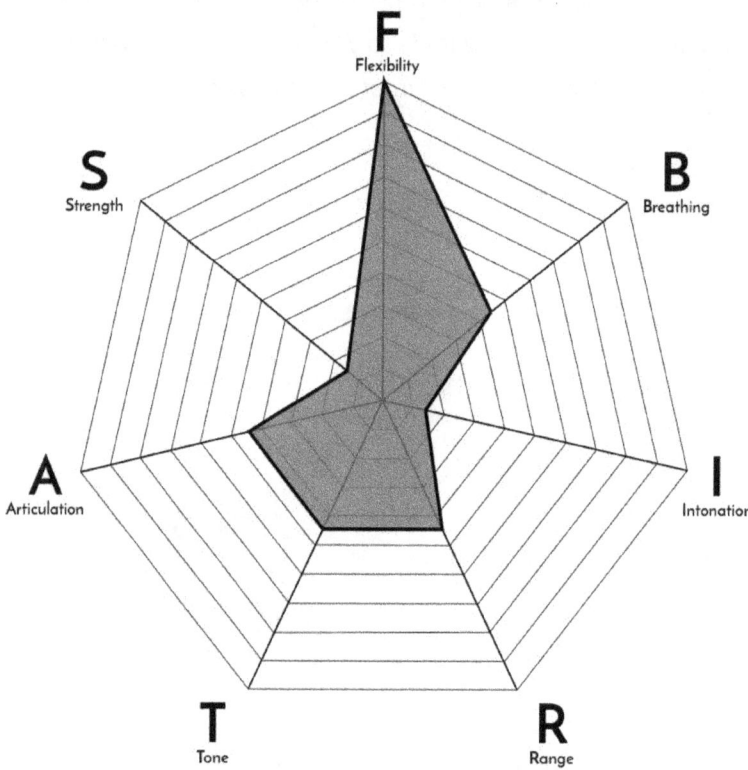

The 7DS graph above displays the relative degree to which the seven dimensions are targeted within a given exercise. As you can see, the exercise in this chapter points to the dimension of flexibility. Most exercises used to warmup the voice will show a high degree of flexibility, but may also target other dimensions such as intonation or range. This all depends on how the exercise is constructed. Later, we will explore how you can customize exercises to target the dimensions you wish to improve upon.

The Throga Technique

Take a small inhalation through your nose, as if sniffing a flower, and begin with a quiet "M" sound on a comfortable high note in your head or falsetto register. Using a higher vocal register (discussed more in Chapter VI, *Range: 4th Dimension*) requires the folds to thin, and the "M" sound puts the mouth and lips in a closed position, creating "backpressure" against the airflow. Backpressure makes it easier for the folds to stretch and start vibrating because it reduces the amount of pressure directly against the folds. This is an essential ingredient when it comes to targeting the dimension of Flexibility. You can also bring the tip of the tongue forward, gently touching your bottom lip, to discourage you from pulling the tongue back to help control the airflow while navigating through your range.

Next, open the "M" into a clear sounding "ē" formant, as in the word "see". Just after creating the ē, slide the note down as far as you can, moving through any available vocal registers. The sliding action from one note to another should have a siren-sounding effect. This type of pattern is known as a "glissando." The shape of the "ē" formant allows the condition of the folds to be heard a bit more clearly than the "M", while still providing a small amount of backpressure.

Finally, at the very end of the descending note, add a lazy and gravelly sound called a "vocal fry." Vocal fry is the tonal texture you might make when you first wake up in the morning or use as a stylistic choice to make a lyric sound more conversational (not applied in classical genres). This creaky-door sound is the by-product of the folds vibrating irregularly and is fairly easy to access on lower notes by spending less air. Although it may sound strange, utilizing this underwhelming amount of air pressure can be used to gently vibrate and loosen the folds. Since this entire exercise lasts only a few seconds on each breath, you can rest and repeat it many times in the same range of notes while applying the *Throga Guidelines*.

To hear an example of this exercise and the many exercises in the following chapters, please refer to the 🔊 **7DS Book Media** on the

Throga website. When vocalizing with this or other tracks, be sure to adapt your voice to any octave, whether that be high or low, that feels easy and tension free.

Now returning backstage, Jack's voice was responding so much better. This suggests that the vocal folds gained elasticity and that the swelling had been potentially reduced, and now he was ready to move on in his warmup. Gradually, Jack advanced to louder volumes and more open vowel formations. Then came a knock at the door.

Showtime.

Flexibility is a vital step in your ability to sing well and to sing often, but stretching alone won't actually make you a better singer. For example, imagine you were to try learning a new dance move, maybe the "Moonwalk." If you were to loosen your muscles by stretching your legs and feet, yes, you'd be less likely to injure yourself. But without ever practicing the coordination and timing of the related muscles, you wouldn't suddenly be able to do the dance!

So now we've talked about warming up warmed up and being flexible, let's explore the next dimension so that we can develop and improve upon the coordination and efficiency of how we breathe.

Flexibility Summary

- *Flexibility* refers to the pliability of the vocal folds.

- Warmups should always begin with the dimension of *flexibility* in mind.

- Your vocal folds must be hydrated throughout the day to stay loose and flexible.

- Inside the larynx, the vocal folds consist of five layers, which are used to vibrate and create sound.

- To target *flexibility* in training, focus on low volumes, closed formants, and quick pattern exercises.

- Vocal responsiveness will help you access whatever your current singing skills are.

- Aside from vocal rest, *flexibility* should be targeted for greater periods of time when dealing with fatigue, head colds, or allergies.

Breathing: 2nd Dimension

Chapter IV

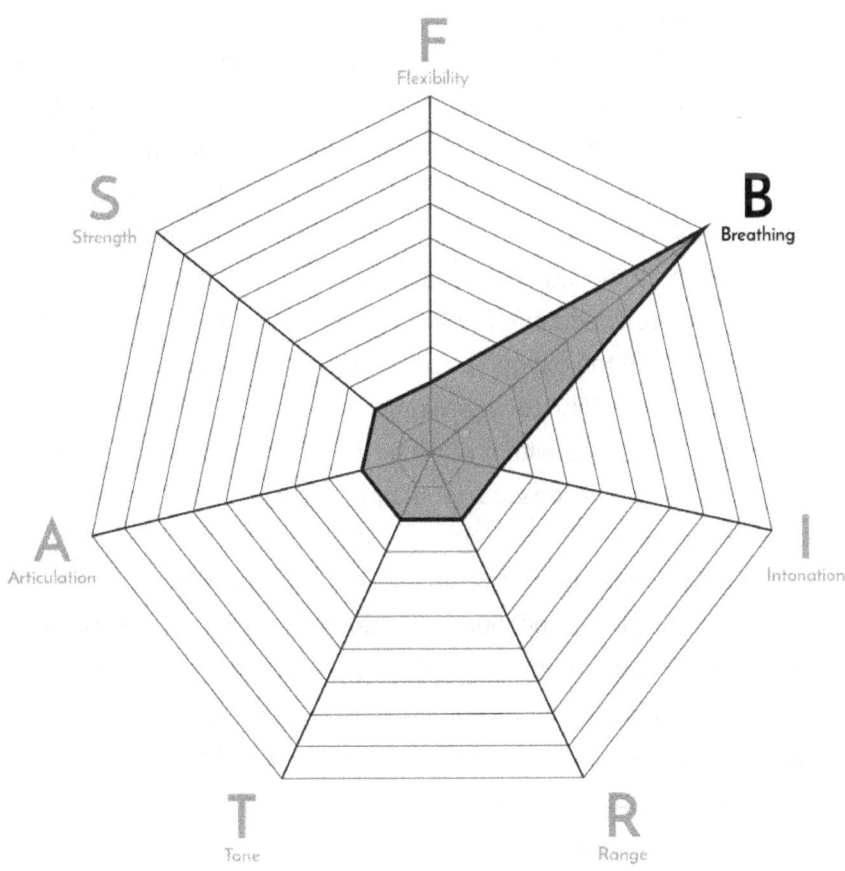

Breathing: The control of our breath

We can go weeks without consuming food, roughly seven days without water, and yet, only MINUTES without oxygen. This goes to show how essential breathing and oxygen are to our survival. Our bodies prioritize the need for oxygen over our love for singing. So it's best to understand and work with the body's natural patterns and behaviors when doing so.

Scientifically, breathing is the process of taking air into the lungs, absorbing the available oxygen, and releasing carbon dioxide back into the air. The lungs can be thought of as two large sponges, with tissue made of hundreds of millions of tiny balloon-like air sacs called alveoli. Alveoli are responsible for this absorption of oxygen into the bloodstream so that it can be distributed throughout the body. Carbon dioxide is then released into our lungs through the same process and as a by-product of the oxygen used. However, in relation to producing sound, it is our ability to coordinate the muscles responsible for managing air pressure within our instrument. This management can be divided into two processes: inhalation and exhalation, breathing in and breathing out.

As we touched upon in *How Your Instrument Works*, when the inhalation muscles around our lungs contract, it creates a vacuum, causing a rush of air, made up of about 20% oxygen, to pass through the larynx and into our lungs. To create that vacuum, the diaphragm contracts and flexes downward. This action displaces our internal organs, causing our stomach region to expand outward, allowing more room for the lungs to elongate and inflate.

Taking full advantage of the diaphragm's natural function is commonly known as "diaphragmatic breathing." This is easily visible when your body is at rest, about to fall asleep, or when watching an infant lying on her back.

Another important group of muscles used for inhalation is the external intercostal muscles situated between the ribs. When these

The Throga Technique

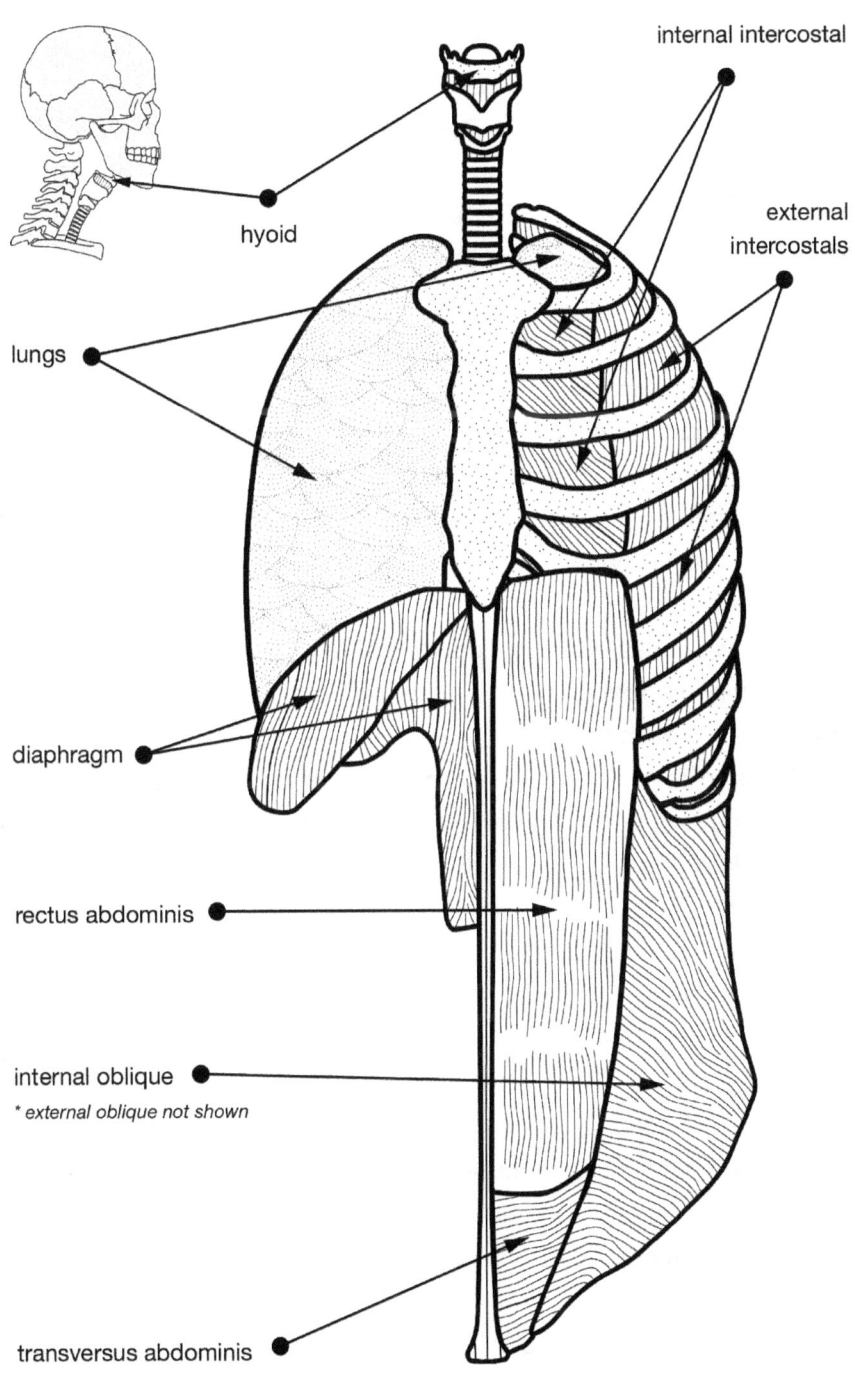

muscles contract on their own, it is often referred to as "chest breathing," because you can see the ribcage flair up and out as they pull on the sides of the lungs. Relying solely on these muscles to sing often stems from poor posture or being overly concerned with how we might appear or sound. Perhaps from sucking in our gut or having abdominal tension. This can put you in a negative chase for more air when singing and disrupt the flow of the song.

The reality is, we rarely need the amount of air we think we do in any given phrase. But not utilizing our diaphragm creates two problems. First, it's difficult to coordinate the muscles around our ribs for efficient breathing. And secondly, the intercostals only provide approximately 30% lung capacity. The diaphragm, on the other hand, is responsible for 60%.

That's right, sixty percent!

That is a massive sacrifice to make if your body is tense or responding to poor behaviors when trying to sing. If you're wondering about the remaining 10%, it can be achieved by stretching the top of the lungs in response to lifting your shoulders. However, this extra percentage isn't worth the regional neck tension that coincides, as it tends to interfere with the freedom for singing.

So why are we talking so much about the process of inhalation instead of exhalation, which is what we actually use to produce sound? Because the quality of your inhale directly affects the quality of your exhale. In order to release the air in our lungs, the inhalation muscles have to disengage, allowing the lungs to deflate. The exhalation muscles are then used to help create a balanced or intentional amount of air pressure underneath the vocal folds. This is known as "subglottic pressure." Additionally, they can squeeze the lungs beyond the body's rested state to help with the recoil action into the next breath, as well as to increase subglottic pressure to trigger desired sounds and tonal qualities that we might be after. This should generally be done sparingly with a minimal approach, relative to the style and genre to avoid stress and fatigue.

The exhalation muscles include the abdominal muscles (external and internal obliques, transversus abdominis, and rectus abdominis) and *internal* intercostal muscles. Given the sheer size and strength of these collective muscles, it's understandable how even the slightest adjustment or contraction can overwhelm the very small muscles of the larynx. To accurately sing the note we want, at the correct volume, using the vowel and tone we intended, will partially rely on our ability to control our airflow well.

Though we all may struggle with this coordination from time to time, some singers appreciate the need for efficient breath control on a much deeper level. Brianna is one such person. At just 10 years old, Brianna lives with a very complicated and deadly disease known as cystic fibrosis (CF). Normally, our lungs produce a thin layer of mucus that helps protect the airways from dangerous bacteria that can cause infections. For those with CF, a genetic condition that primarily affects the lungs, the body produces thick, sticky mucus instead. This mucus then builds up in the airways and becomes a source of infection and inflammation, and often it leads to severe damage, scarring, and poor lung function over an extended period of time.

You may experience a similar inability to exchange oxygen during an asthma attack or when battling a cold with severe chest congestion. In addition to the constant vocal fold irritation caused by having to clear your throat, you're left with a sensation of not being able to get enough air, even though you are clearly expanding your lungs. Those millions of tiny alveoli are unable to bud easily; tricking the brain into believing the body needs to take another breath. As a vocalist, this will not only shorten our phrasing, it will make it very difficult to manage the air needed to trigger the vocal folds accurately.

Despite this obstacle, Brianna defies the very expectations of her disease with an incredible display of vocal strength, range, and skill.

This was made quite evident at MetLife Stadium, when her performance of the National Anthem was received by tens of thousands of people cheering her on during a live NFL season broadcast.

How does she do it?

Certainly, her fearlessness plays a significant role in her success, but it's her ability to manage whatever air she has available in the moment that allows her to execute her intentions so well. And it's that efficiency and minimization from which we can all benefit. Breathing exercises that help achieve this will challenge the management of air while phonating, the vibrating of the folds, rather than concentrating on only the air itself. Rapid "Hē" triplets on single notes, is a perfect example.

The Throga Technique

Breathing Exercise
(Rapid "Hē" triplets on a single note)

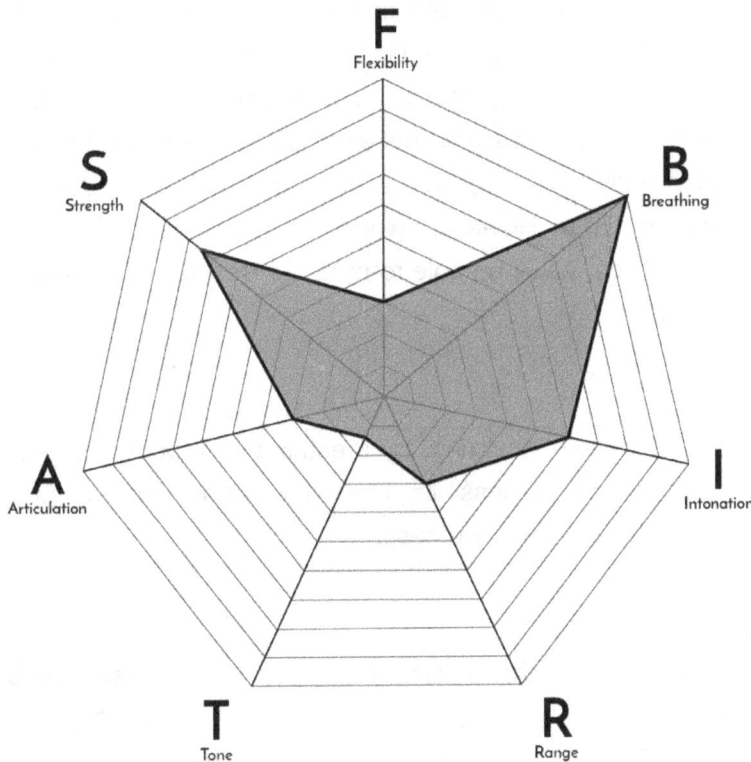

This exercise utilizes the "H" consonant. When you produce an "H", your vocal folds are positioned slightly apart from each other, yet close enough to resist the airflow passing between them. The use of the "H" as part of an exercise has been popular in vocal training for hundreds of years due to this unique posturing. In the right context, it can help you address several vocal dimensions at once, namely *breathing*, *intonation,* and *strength*.

To explore this, try repeating a "Hē" sound as fast as you can at a quiet volume. Any pitch is fine, just be sure that your abdominals don't pulsate in an effort to force the sound. Since smaller muscles move faster than larger ones, the swift repetition of the folds switching from the non-vibrating "H" position to the vibrating "ē" sound and then back to the "H" again, will help isolate the small intrinsic muscles of the larynx. These laryngeal muscles are responsible for the folds' tension and positioning, known as "approximation." If there's too much or too little air pressure, those smaller muscles won't be able to respond quickly and accurately, resulting in stuttered, delayed, or even absent "H"'s. However, when the air is correctly balanced against the folds, you'll be able to produce "H"s relatively easily at a very quick pace.

> *NOTE:* When vocalizing, try breathing in through just your nose whenever possible. This will help set you up for a natural and relaxed process.

As you'll hear in the *Breathing Exercise* example (🔊 **7DS Book Media**), a rapid triplet pattern is used on single notes. This pattern makes it easy to focus on one grouping of "Hē" sounds at a time. The goal is to have every "H" not only defined, but also consistent in quality, volume, and duration. This way, you'll know if you're spending the air equally from the beginning to the end of each new breath. For example, if you notice the first "H" is louder or longer than the last "H," the air wasn't managed as efficiently as it could have been. Also, be sure to aim for a clear tone and steady volume during all of the "ē" sounds as well.

If at any point the "H" becomes undefined, or if a whispery sound overlaps into the "ē," it suggests that an imbalance took place. Presuming you've warmed-up, are well hydrated, and in good health, the imbalance is one of two things: you overspent your air or had trouble coordinating the small muscles in charge of approximating the vocal folds. Either way, this can be a valuable exercise if you tend to run out of breath or fatigue easily.

If you find that the exercise itself causes a feeling of fatigue, there's a good chance that you're unintentionally stressing your instrument. The body often does this whenever we try something new, like when first learning to tie our shoes or eat with chopsticks. Our movements can be awkward and stiff, making it difficult for subtle and effortless adjustments. If this happens, simply pause the exercise, have a sip of water, and try a couple of *flexibility* exercises to loosen up for a moment before returning to the *breathing* exercise.

If the exercise isn't sounding right to you and you're feeling frustrated, try temporarily replacing the "H" with an "S" feature. Exercise "features" are a distinguishable disruption of a formant or tonal pattern, which modifies the functionality of the exercise in same way. In the case of an "S" feature, the position of the tongue will assist by regulating the amount of air being spent and alleviating some of the subglottic pressure leading into the "ē."

This modification can be likened to helping a child stay upright when first learning to ride a two-wheeled bike. When they're ready, you let go of the seat while in motion, so that they can try and balance the bike on their own. Following this analogy, you can start with "Sē" when first learning or troubleshooting the exercise. Then when you're ready, release your tongue into a "Hē" to try and balance it with each new note.

There are many ways to challenge and tackle this dimension. We'll take a look at other possibilities a little later on. In the meantime, it might seem a little overwhelming with everything you have to remember already when vocalizing. Take a deep breath and take your time towards establishing a high degree of breath control. It will ultimately assist in developing a strong foundation for all of the other dimensions to come.

Breathing Summary

- Good breath control makes it easier to balance other dimensions.

- *Breathing* can be broken down into two processes: inhalation and exhalation.

- For singing, *breathing* refers to the control of air pressure within the vocal instrument.

- Your body's need for oxygen overrides your desire to sing.

- Diaphragmatic breathing allows for more lung capacity and ease of control.

- The quality of your inhale directly affects the quality of your exhale.

- It's best to do exercises that include the vibration of the folds, rather than just the management of air on it's own.

Intonation: 3rd Dimension

Chapter V

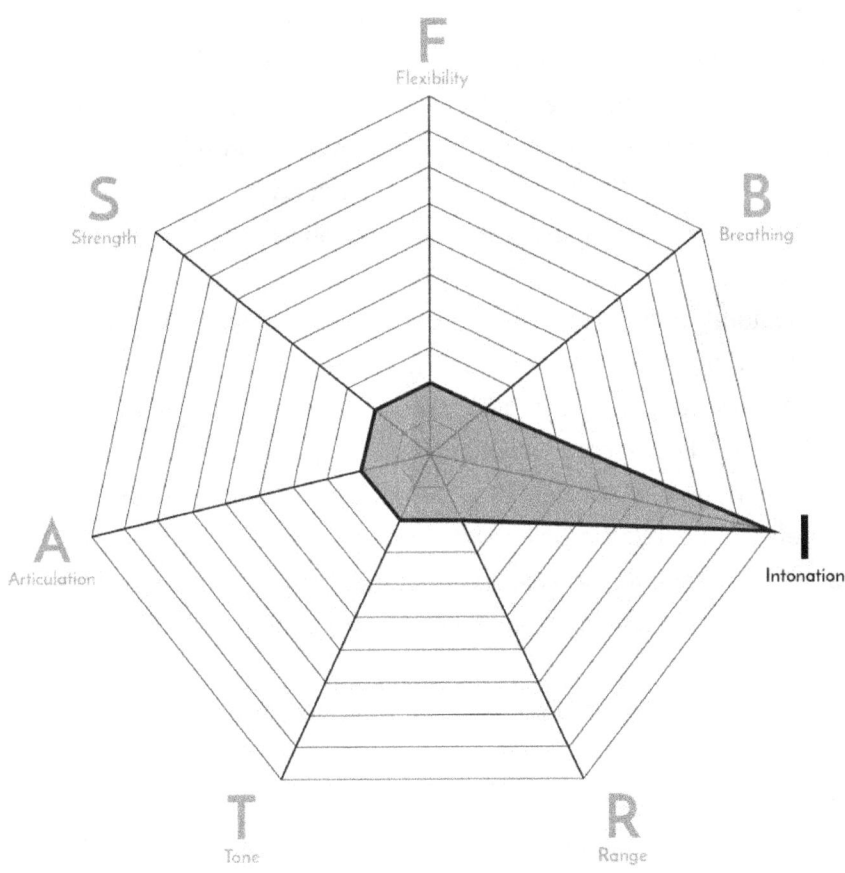

Intonation: The control of our pitch

We've all kicked a ball around at one time or another. The backyard is freshly mowed, your big brother or a best friend runs way back, and in your head, you envision the ball in slow motion soaring over the clothesline, between the trees, and landing perfectly at his feet. So you line up the shot, give it everything you have, smashing your foot into the back of the ball, only to look up to see it going straight over the fence and into the neighbor's thorn bushes.

Most of us too, have shared that same experience when we sing; forcing too much air with too much tension in an effort to "hit" the notes of a song. We may occasionally get it right and sing every note we were aiming for, but it won't happen consistently without practice and proper coordination.

Naturally, your skills will improve, at least to some extent, just by exploring your voice over time. The same can be said for any other physical activity, like playing soccer on the weekends with your friends and family. However, professional soccer players can place the ball where, when, and how fast they want it, and under difficult conditions. Whether chipping the ball a short distance or crossing it to the other side of the field, the finesse and command over the ball in the context of a game are very much like the control over the pitch in the context of a melody.

Intonation, the third dimension, refers to our ability to match the intended pitches of a scale or melody. A pitch, or musical note, is a labeled description of a specific. When an object vibrates at a constant speed, it creates a sound wave that is both measurable and relatively easy to identify. For example, when a felt hammer strikes the middle string of a tuned piano, the string vibrates 261.6 times per second, which we have labeled "C4." When you reproduce that frequency with your voice by vibrating the outer layers of your vocal folds at the exact same speed, you are singing "in tune" with the piano. Let's examine further as to how we're able to arrive at such precise speeds of vibration with our instrument.

Your vocal folds, only about half the size of your eyelids, hinge from just behind the bump in the front of your throat, the thyroid cartilage, and open into a V shape to the rear of the larynx when relaxed. To create a pitch, the folds come together and stretch horizontally against the airflow to create tension, similarly to how the strings of a piano or guitar are tightened and stretched when being tuned. The muscles predominantly responsible for creating this tension are the cricothyroids. They tilt the thyroid cartilage forward, causing the folds to stretch in an antagonistic relationship with another set of muscles, the thyroarytenoids, which contract with an opposing force, shortening or relaxing the folds.

Given how small these muscles are, you might imagine how little effort it takes to make a significant impact on the "tuning" of your voice. Those who are able to consistently and accurately jump from one note to another, transitioning intervals, in any vocal register, have excellent *intonation* skills. It's the same as a soccer player with fancy footwork, effortlessly navigating through his opponents on the way to scoring a goal, just as it was rehearsed a thousand times before. The rest of us, who might struggle with coordinating the muscles related to *intonation*, may have to spend more quality time honing in on this dimension over others in order to balance the instrument as a whole.

Practicing a song over and over again is beneficial, but more effort may be necessary to improve overall pitch control. Engaging other senses by feeling or seeing the vibration of our folds can help greatly in the acceleration of singing in tune. A chromatic guitar tuner, for instance, is a perfect tool for this, as it will display whatever frequency or pitch is detected.

While watching a tuner, you can slide your voice up and down until your preferred note appears. Triggering your visual cortex, the part of the brain that processes the sense of sight, will help guide you, not only to sing in tune, but also to provide a heightened awareness

7 Dimensions of Singing

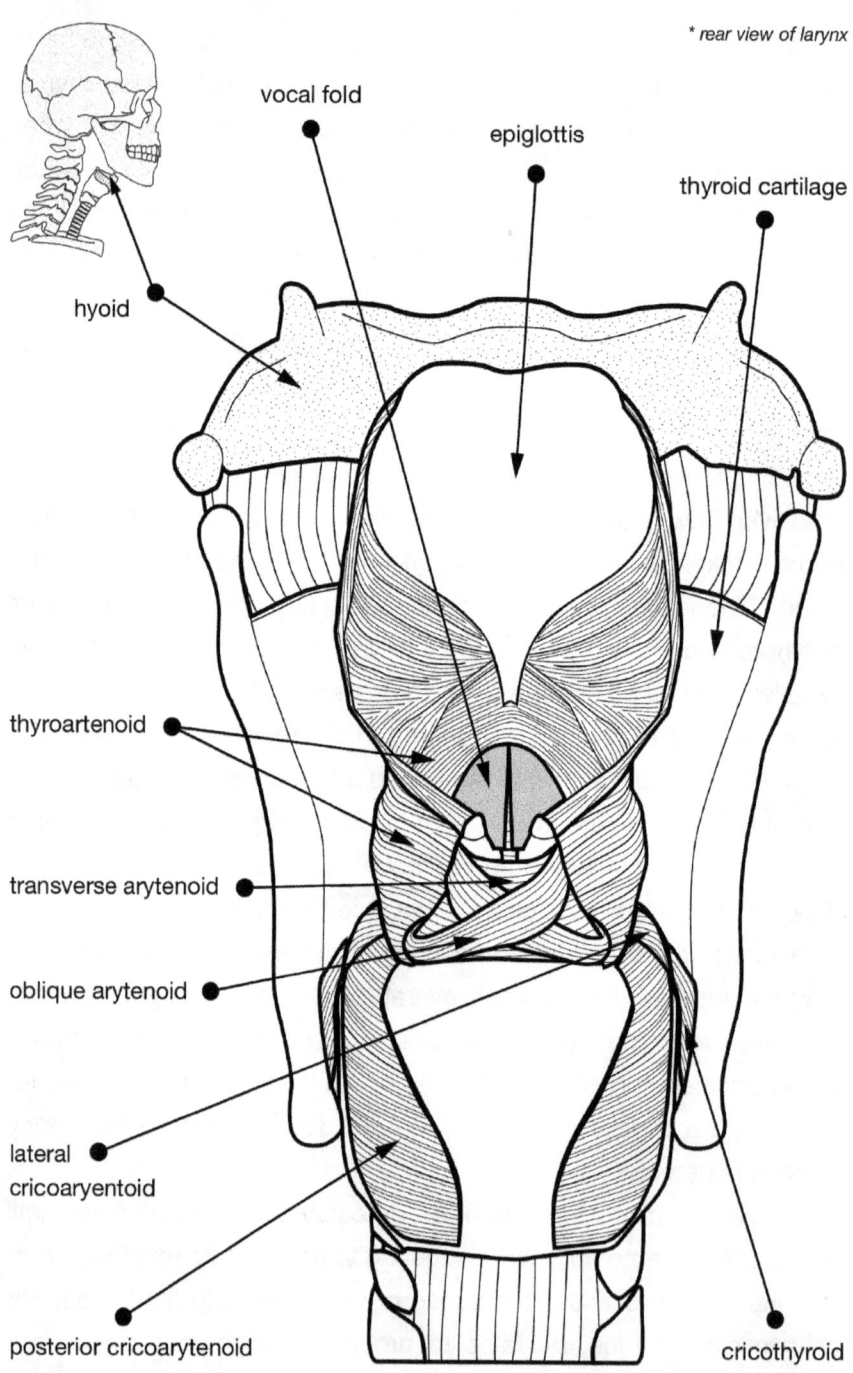

*rear view of larynx

The Throga Technique

to the speed of vibration in your body. Though it may be a slow and tedious process at first, the more sensory feedback you have, the quicker you're going to progress. Once you can consistently match pitches, there are more specialized exercises for coordinating the muscles associated with *intonation*, such as doing "z pulses."

Intonation Exercise
("z" pulse scales)

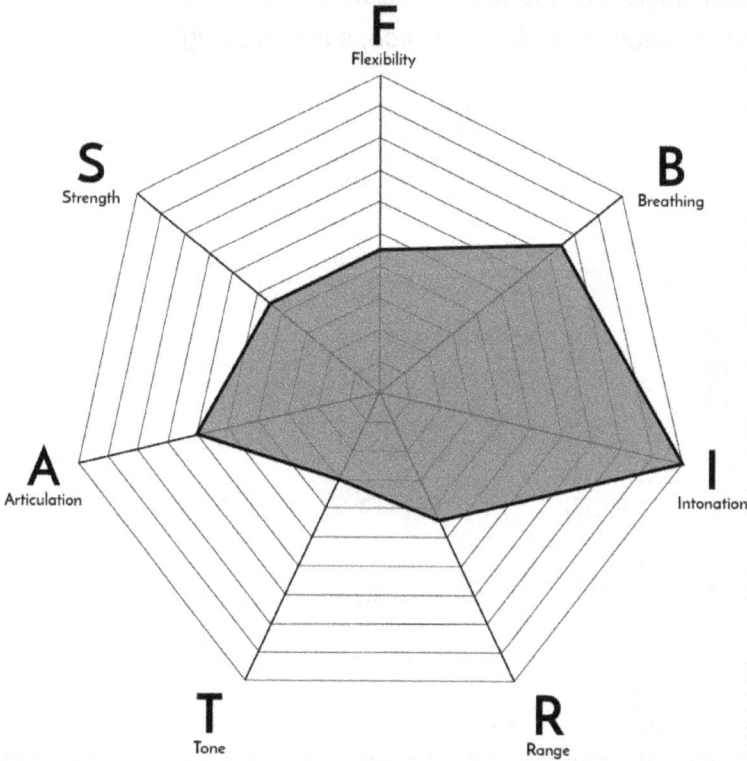

This exercise utilizes a "z", which is a very unique formant that maintains a close relationship between the dimensions of *intonation* and *breathing*. Because of this relationship, it's best to address the management of breath before we introduce the pitches.

Upon a gentle release of air, place your tongue very lightly against the roof of the mouth, known as the hard palate. This action generates a hissing sound called a "fricative" and allows you to hear and feel the steadiness of the airflow independent of any vocal fold activity. Once you're able to regulate the hiss with a steady stream of air, vocalize a

The Throga Technique

comfortable pitch anywhere in your typical speaking range. This should create a steady buzzing sound.

The simultaneous vibration of the vocal folds inside the larynx, with the fricative against the hard palate, provides two clearly identifiable and sustainable sounds to monitor. This is what makes the "z" such an interesting and challenging formant to work with. When done correctly, it will alert you to any imbalance taking place.

As soon as you're comfortable creating a sustained "z," you can introduce the "pulse" portion of the exercise. To do this, rotate back and forth between the "z" and the "hiss," for one beat each, on a single breath. The challenge here is to target the muscles that bring the folds together on your desired note and then to separate them, without disturbing the hissing sound. The muscles responsible for bringing the folds together, a process known as "adduction," are the transverse, lateral, and oblique arytenoids. The muscles responsible for separating the folds, known as "abduction," are the posterior arytenoids. By isolating these muscles, in relation to the cricothyroids and thyroarytenoids, which adjust the tension of the folds, you're essentially turning the folds "on and off." You can think of this action as a target practice for pitches.

Aside from providing some auditory feedback, the fricative's primary function is to make sure that the tongue doesn't pull back or modify its position to aid in the management of your selected pitches. If the "hiss" is interrupted, stutters, or changes in quality or volume, it lets you know that an imbalance took place. This is a red flag because we don't want the tongue muscles involved with managing your airflow or assisting in the dimension of *intonation*. We want those muscles fully available for other dimensions discussed in later chapters.

It's time to try a little vocal-soccer of your own. Go to the 🔊 **7DS Book Media** and listen to the *Intonation Exercise* example to hear exactly what it should sound like. The pattern used within an

49

exercise plays a big role in helping to target *intonation* because the more complex it is, the more skill may be required to execute it. For this exercise, we're going to do a pattern that uses only the first five notes of a major scale, but it skips around in such a way that makes it a bit tricky. If we were to use numbers instead of the "z", it would read as "1, 3, 2, 4, 3, 5, 3, 4, 2, 3, 1."

It may take several tries to work out the coordination of the "z" before you can apply it to the pattern. So if you're having any trouble, simply spend more time working with single notes at slower speeds for the "z" and practice using numbers with the "practice track" included in the **7DS Book Media**. After some practice, you'll be able to bring them together. For the record, even seasoned professionals struggle with this exercise at first.

> NOTE: *When referring to pitches within a scale or melody, try replacing words like "hit," which has a forceful connotation, with non-tension-triggering words like "sing" or "vocalize."*

How did you do with the practice track?

Were you able to sustain a steady "hiss" independent of the notes? If you're not 100% sure whether you matched the pitches correctly or not, try using a guitar tuner app or practice with a knowledgeable musician or vocal coach to get some feedback.

When you're ready to try more challenging patterns or interested in learning quick vocal riffs or runs, often used in genres such as r&b and opera, practice the pattern or melody you want to learn with a legato "z" very slowly at first. Legato refers to the notes being connected, meaning there is no so no "pulse" action as described in the above exercise. Once you're confident with the accuracy of the notes in slow motion, increase the tempo little by little until it's quick and defined enough to try it with the lyrics. Some riffs may take a few minutes to lock in while others may take a few months of practice. This all depends on your skill level, how complicated the note pattern is, and how efficiently you train.

And just a quick note, let's address the illusion that this dimension is more important than others. Unfortunately, most of today's popular music is saturated with artificially modified voices. It creates a false standard of what is expected of the instrument in terms of pitch accuracy. Singing pitch-perfect is wonderful IF you are still able to convey the emotional intent of the lyrics.

Listen closely to some of the most successful and revered singers in history and you will hear that their performances are riddled with imperfect pitches. The "greats" weren't great because they were always in tune. They were great because they were able to make you feel. Singers like Elvis Presley, Billie Holiday, Freddie Mercury, Patsy Cline, Whitney Houston, Kurt Cobain, Etta James, David Bowie, Janis Joplin, Frank Sinatra, Michael Jackson, Karen Carpenter, Bob Marley, Joan Sutherland, Judy Garland, and Ray Charles all took advantage of their voices being a fretless instrument. They realized the control of their pitch was just one component to help them deliver their intended emotion or story.

The point of bringing this up is not to discourage the value of singing accurate frequencies, but for us to recognize that there is no one dimension of the voice that is more important than the others. The more equalized dimensions become in your practice, the more choices you have to lean on in the execution of your artistry.

Intonation Summary

- *Intonation* is the control of your pitch and ability to go from one note to another.

- Avoid the idea of "hitting" notes and "sing" or "vocalize" them instead.

- To sing "in tune," is to match the speed of vibration of the note you want with your vocal folds.

- Loosening or tensing the vocal folds in order to alter their speed of vibration against airflow is what creates pitch.

- Your vocal folds are very small and it takes very little effort to adjust notes when using the right muscles.

- When training, try using a visual aid like a guitar tuner or vocal app to verify your pitch accuracy.

- You don't need to be perfectly in tune when singing to have a great performance.

Range: 4th Dimension

Chapter VI

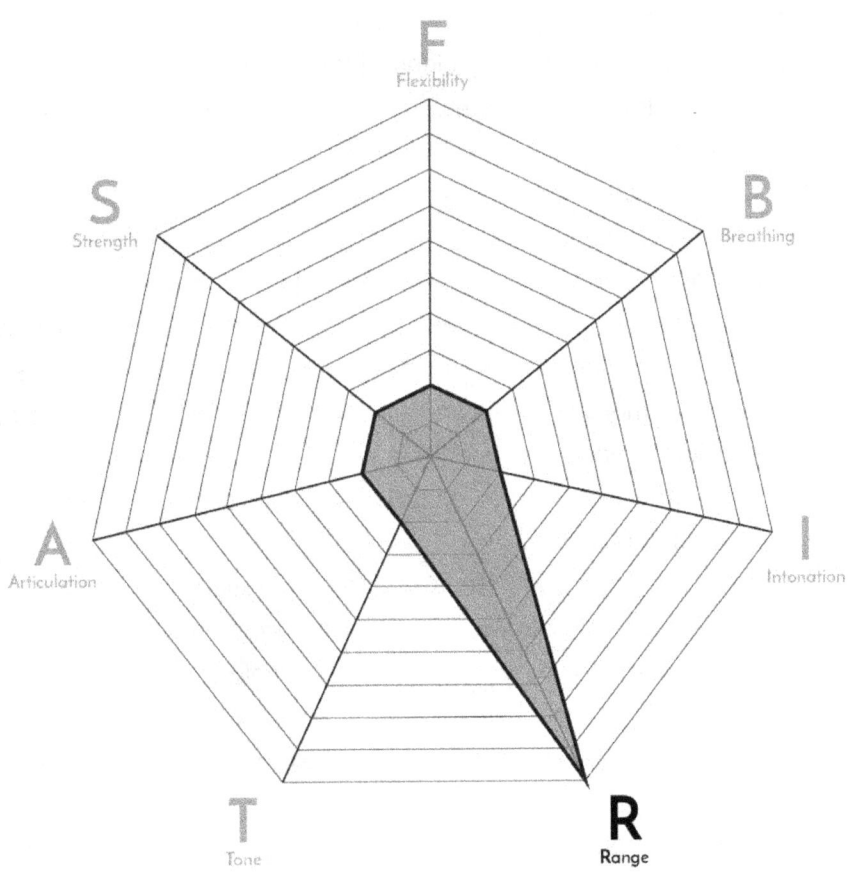

Range: The vocal balance from the lowest to highest note

7 Dimensions of Singing

Did you skip ahead to this chapter? If so, you're not alone. Of all the vocal dimensions, *range* is the one most singers obsess over, and understandably so. However, in most cases, when a singer complains about his range or says he can't reach certain notes within a song, what he means to say is, "I can't get the *sound* I want on certain notes." A high note sung with an intense screeching sound, causing people to cover their ears and clench their teeth, won't provoke the same reaction, if the same note were sung with ease, bathed in soft, soothing, overtones. With that in mind, the dimension of *range* is defined as the coordination and vocal balance of muscles from the lowest to highest note available.

Learning to control and access one's full vocal range is a lot like learning how to control one's speed and ability to shift gears smoothly on a bicycle. Knowing when and how to transition between gears, without jerking the bike or having to compensate with more effort, takes coordination and practice. Peddling hard in the wrong gear will not only limit how fast you can go, but it's also a waste of energy and can fatigue you quickly.

When singing, the vocal folds' speed of vibration determines the pitch; the slower they vibrate, the lower the frequency. In turn, the faster they vibrate, the higher the frequency. If your folds were to stay at a constant mass (thickness), they would only be able to vibrate within a limited range of notes based on their length and your ability to tense them.

The same limitations will take place for a cyclist on a bike with only one gear. Multiple gears provide a variety of choices based on the terrain, the distance, the bike condition, and the goals of the cyclist. Although you only have one set of "true" vocal folds to sing with, you can adjust their mass and relative positions to create multiple registers (gears). This is what will help you reach your goals regardless of a song's terrain.

Vocal Registers: The number of vocal registers, terminology, and descriptions is heavily debated among pedagogues. In an effort to communicate the register terms as universally as possible, at least within the confines of this book, let's define them according to the physical position of the vocal folds and their relation to airflow:

(1) "Vocal fry" was earlier described as a vocal texture. It can also be viewed as the lowest register with an irregular vibration of the folds, caused by a lack of subglottic pressure and slight release in the vocal folds' tension. Its name origin comes from the croaky sound it generates.

(2) "Chest" is when the vocal folds are approximated in a thicker position than the head register. Its name origin comes from being able to feel vibration primarily in the chest.

(3) "Head" is when the vocal folds are approximated in a thinner position than the chest register. Its name origin comes from being able to feel a vibration in the head and not the chest.

(4) "Falsetto" is when the vocal folds are in a thinner position than the head register and slightly separated. Its name origin comes from not being able to feel a vibration in either the chest or head.

(5) "Whistle" can be viewed as the highest register, which takes place when the vocal folds are pulled tight with a tiny space for air to travel through, forcing air

molecules to create high-pitched frequencies through non-vibrating folds. Its name origin comes from the similarity to whistling with the lips.

Due to the limitations in being able to project the voice in vocal fry and to articulate words in whistle, the middle three registers are the most commonly referenced. Let's compare a medial cross-section of the vocal folds (showing all five layers discussed in Chapter III, *Flexibility: 1st Dimension*) as we have defined them:

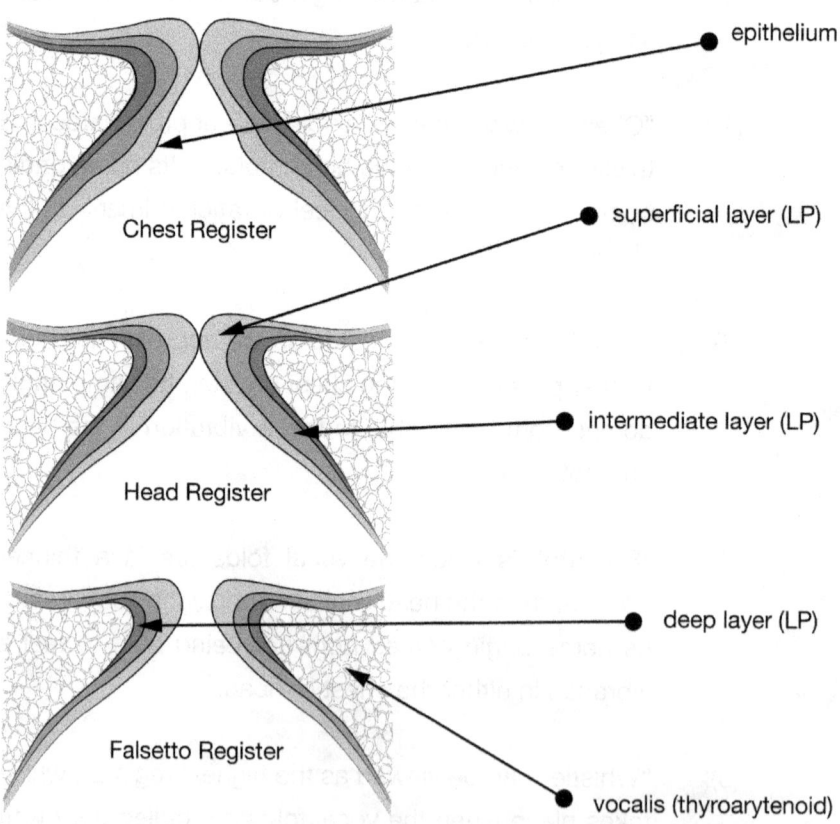

The primary muscles used to determine the mass and approximation of the folds are the thyroarytenoid (vocalis), cricothyroid, and arytenoid muscles. For clarity, the vocalis is often referenced independently from the thyroarytenoid due to its dual role as the deepest layer of the vocal folds. However, these muscles are one in the same and contract as a single unit.

The register transitions are a behavioral phenomenon known as the "passaggio" (aka "mix," "break," or "middle voice"). In regard to position, the passaggio is referring to the percentage of two overlapping registers, as the folds adjust from one relative position to the next against the subglottic pressure. The graph below depicts a basic layout of each register and its overlapping capacities, relative to frequency. You may notice that vocal fry, though difficult to navigate on higher notes, is the only one that can overlap more than two registers. Whereas whistle is unable to overlap even its neighboring register, falsetto. This is due to the nature of how the sounds are produced.

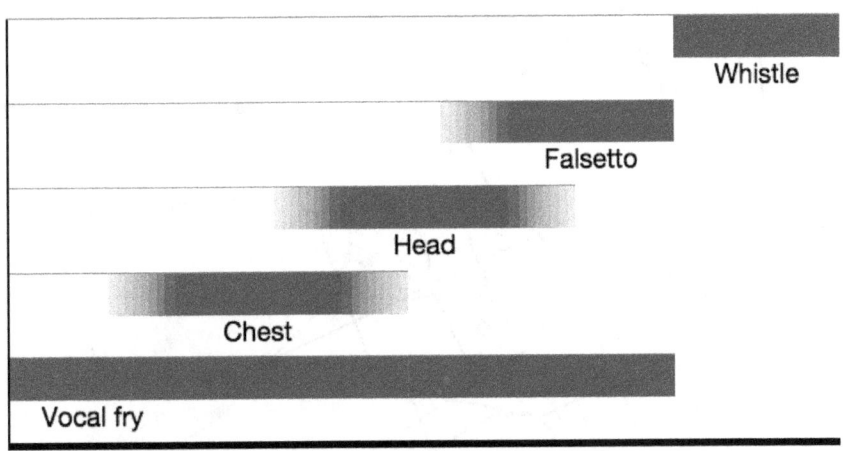

← Frequency (Pitch) →

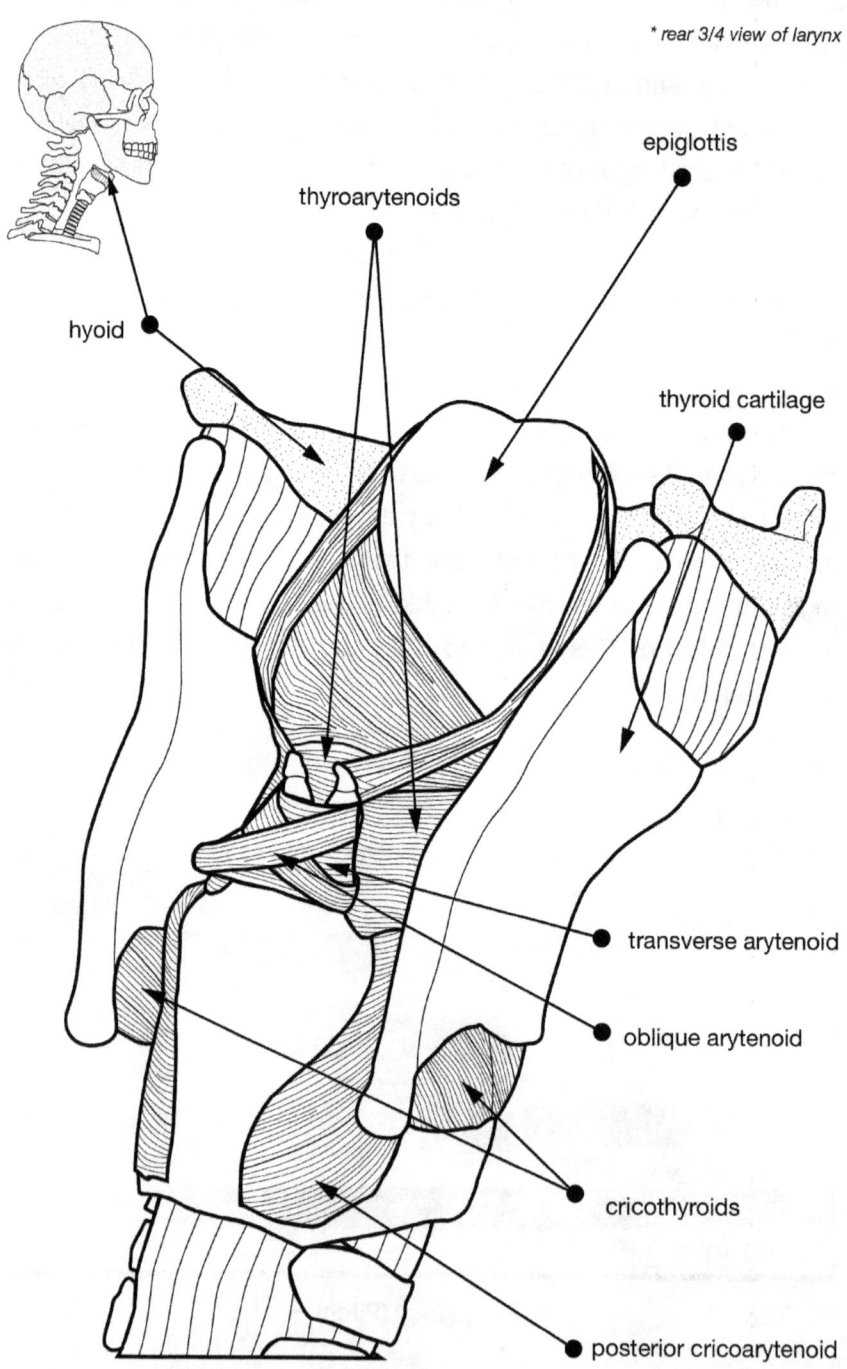

Now that we've defined some key terminology, let's answer the inevitable question; "How can I improve my vocal range?"

Ted Neeley, the star of the 1973 movie, as well as the U.S. and international tours of the Broadway production *Jesus Christ Superstar,* uses glissando-based exercises even into his 80's. To demonstrate his effortlessness in this dimension, he can sing over three octaves at full volume, night after night on tour.

A glissando, as you may recall, is when you intentionally slide from one note to another. However, this time, we're going to do them slowly and at increasingly louder volumes, which requires both pliability AND stability of the voice. It's no coincidence that *range* is listed in the very center of the dimensions, halfway between *flexibility* and *strength*.

Range Exercise
(Slow "ä" glissandos)

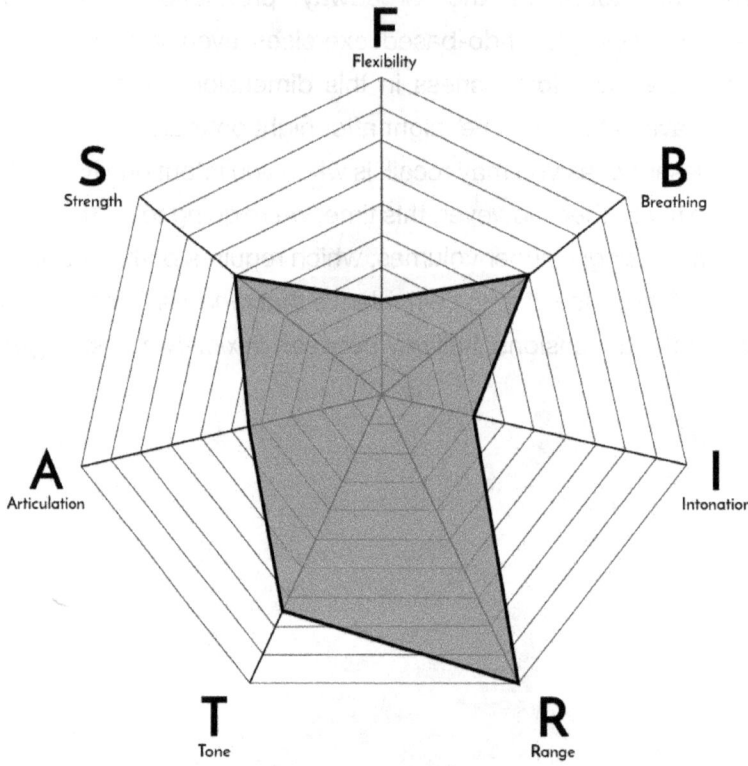

The *Range Exercise* (🔊 **7DS Book Media**) uses a unique pattern that starts in the middle of an octave. It slides downward from the fifth interval to the root note, up to the eighth, and then back to the starting note. The complexity of this pattern invites you to move back and forth between the registers more often than most traditional glissando patterns. Creating opportunities to practice the balance between registers is essential in developing *range*. To target this dimension even further, we will use an open "ä" formant, as in the word "father."

The Throga Technique

This formant dilates the throat and removes any resistance above the larynx, making it harder to mask any imbalances.

To help visualize our goal, think of your chest register as thick blue strings on the left end of the piano and your head register as thin red strings on the right end. Your objective would then be to play as many shades of "purple" as possible, transitioning from the blue strings to red strings, without altering how hard or soft you strike the keys. To skillfully work through this metaphorical passaggio of color, you will need to develop balanced behaviors. So do your best not to avoid or skip over any "purple strings" by altering the volume, adding throat tension, or getting stuck in any one register.

It's important to recognize that your control over volume can be separate from the pitch. If your volume remains constant, it will take LESS air to sing a higher note than a lower one. This is because the greater the air pressure, the more likely the muscles inside your larynx will respond by thickening the folds, making it increasingly difficult to vibrate at faster speeds. It is recommended to try the exercise at a steady quiet volume at first. Only after you're able to successfully navigate from your lowest to highest note with good form, should you increase the overall volume in order to take on a higher level of difficulty.

Keep in mind, that no matter how awkward it may sound, transitioning between registers causes ZERO harm to your folds. Meaning, if you feel any ache or strain when your voice is about to crack, that tension and discomfort aren't because your folds are skipping from one register to another. It comes from you trying to avoid or mask the cracking sound from happening.

If you find yourself skipping a lot of notes, getting frustrated, or experiencing discomfort, try changing the "ä" to a less open formant, such as "ē" or "m." You can always return to the open "ä" once you get more accustomed to the exercise. Otherwise, adding tension in an attempt to steer through your passaggio is like trying to pedal forward on a bike while squeezing the handbrakes at the same time.

This sort of imbalance is often the case for inexperienced singers and those going through puberty. The neurological recalibrations necessary when trading in our single geared kid-bike for a multi-geared adult-sized bike can be frustrating. Our sense of timing and balance is dramatically thrown off with the change in tire size and higher center of gravity. It takes time for our mind and body to adapt, just as it does when our larynx quickly changes size due to hormonal growth spurts in our teens.

The reason many adults continue to struggle with this transition post-puberty is because they never allowed themselves to adapt to the changes in their instrument. Imagine if you were to spend the rest of your life pedaling an adult-sized bike in single gears and you never learned to transition between them. You would always feel awkward and riddled with limitations. This is especially true for those who are, or were as a child, easily embarrassed and emotionally guarded when their speaking or singing voice might crack in front of others.

You don't have to be a daredevil. But you also can't spend your life being afraid to fall off your bike every once in a while, and still expect that you're going to get better and improve.

You need to let it happen.

Laugh it off.

And get back up.

Range Summary

- *Range* is the coordination and vocal balance from lowest to highest note available.

- Coordinating the transition between registers is key to developing and accessing one's full range.

- The mass of the vocal folds can thin to accommodate faster speeds of vibration.

- There are five vocal registers definable by vocal fold position and their relationship with air pressure: vocal fry, chest, head, falsetto, and whistle.

- At a constant volume, higher notes require less air pressure than lower notes.

- *Range* exercises often include large interval patterns at slow tempos or loud volumes.

- Don't be afraid of the awkward "cracking" sound when working through the passaggio.

7 Dimensions of Singing

Tone: 5th Dimension

Chapter VII

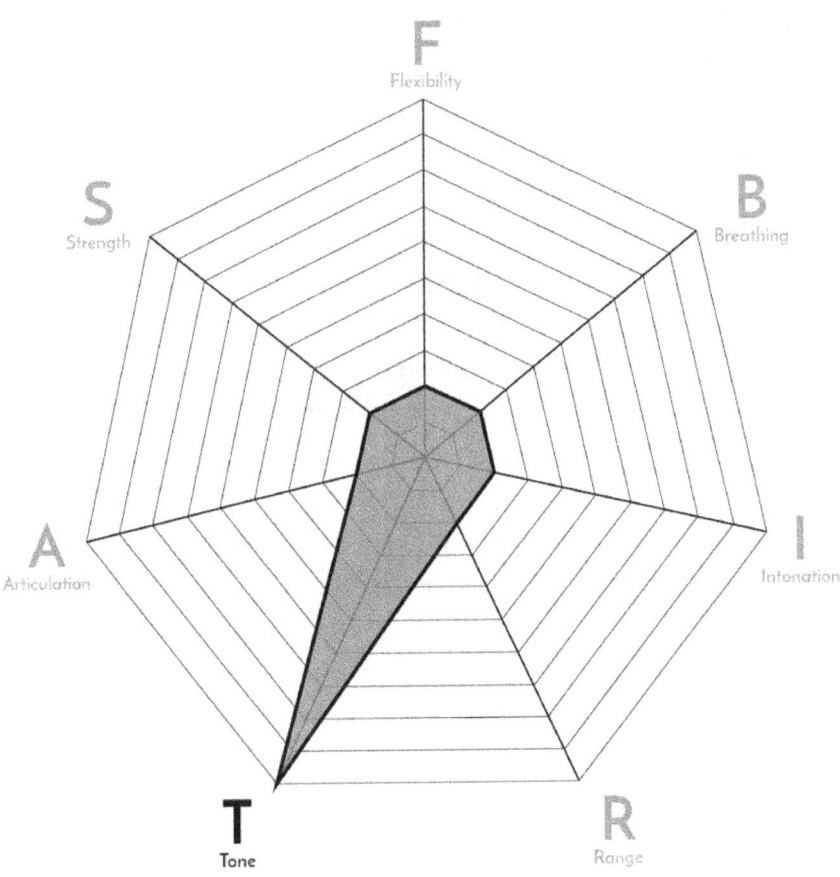

Tone: The quality of sound

7 Dimensions of Singing

"Don't take that tone of voice with me!"

We've ALL heard this growing up. If you're a parent, you've likely repeated it yourself a few times as well. But what does "tone of voice" mean exactly? And why does it matter?

If little Susie says to you "I finished my dinner. Can I please have a cookie?" You would be inclined to say, "Yes, you may." And why not? Susie's plate is in fact empty, and she said, "Please," without grabbing the cookie first. The only thing is, Susie's tone of voice was omitted from this story. What if she was using harsh grunted sounds, at a loud volume, implying a demand for your attention and immediate response? You may not be so keen to say, "Yes."

In another example, imagine you called a friend of yours, Jonathan, to chat casually about what happened the night before. But as soon as he answered your call with, "Hello," you felt your heart race and a knot deepening in the pit of your stomach with every fleeting moment, literally holding your breath, waiting to hear what he'll say next.

Why would your body respond so dramatically like that? All he said was, "Hello." This time, the omitted tone of voice told a different story. Jonathan sounded like he was getting choked up and about to burst into tears. Your mind's emotional center analyzed the characteristics of his voice BEFORE you even had a chance to process the information consciously. Now your thoughts are swimming with scenarios of what might have happened and what you'll be able to do about it.

Does this timeline seem familiar? It's the same sequence of events that took our ancestors thousands of years to refine. Each one of us re-lives this history in our own stages of learning from the time we're born. First, we learn to diagnose and respond to *tone*, whether the sound is something to run from, run towards, or ignore. Next, we process and rationalize the sound along with any other bits of environmental information available. Meanwhile, our intuitive responses have been set in motion, causing various physical forms of action and communication.

This is why *tone*, the fifth dimension, is so important to understand and use to our advantage. The authenticity of your words or lyrics will only be validated if the quality of your voice reflects the same emotional intent. Like wearing the right makeup to match your mood and attire, it makes for a much more striking and memorable impression.

Yet, so far, we've only discussed *tone* at the surface. Anyone can mimic the qualities of a voice that imply if you're sad, happy, angry, or surprised, regardless of whether or not it's sincere. But what about your "core" tone? Your sonic fingerprint underneath the surface, which makes you identifiably different from a sea of others. Is that sound genetic? If you read the *Introduction*, you already know the answer.

No.

You've spent your entire life subconsciously defining the unique timbre and vocal characteristics you have today, and only a percentage of it can be argued as genetic. Voice-over artists and impressionists, such as Michael Winslow and the late Robin Williams, demonstrated these skills throughout their careers by exquisitely mimicking other voices, dialects, instruments, and noises. Their degree of tonal coordination is perplexing for sure, but it's not magic. A skilled impressionist has highly developed communication between thought and vocal tract. If you suspend your disbelief long enough, you'll start to realize something amazing within your own voice as well; if YOU created your sound, then that would also have to mean that YOU can change it.

If you're happy with the sound of your voice throughout your entire range, fantastic! Keep reading to learn more about *tone* and how you can manipulate it, should you ever choose to do so (or are instructed to by a director or producer). If, on the other hand, you think your voice sounds too "nasally," "thin," "cartoony," "strained," "light," "harsh", "masculine," or "feminine," know that it is within your control. You can modify the sound of your voice in certain moments of a song or throughout an entire performance. In order to do this, we need to first understand where and how *tone* is created.

Tone is a result of the resonant patterns (amplified frequencies) within a given space, known as the resonator. Every instrument has one: the body of a guitar, the soundboard of a piano, and the hollow space of a drum. The material(s) used to create the space also play a vital role. The density and mass of an alloy or the coarseness of the wood will highlight or dampen various frequencies, allowing us to identify the difference between a saxophone and a clarinet, even if they were to play the same melody at the same time. The vocal instrument's resonator starts inside the larynx, just above the folds, and extends upwards into a very malleable space defined by pharyngeal walls.

The pharynx is made of cylindrically shaped constrictor muscles, divided into three distinguishable parts. The first, and most tonally influential regarding our core sound, is the space directly above the larynx named the laryngopharynx, also known as hypopharyngeal. Sound is amplified in this region and moves upwards to the oropharynx. You can see this by looking into a mirror with an open mouth. Lastly, is the nasopharynx at the very top of the throat, which opens into the nasal cavities for additional high-frequency resonance. *Tone* can also be manipulated and fine-tuned within the oral cavity, formed by the tongue, jaw (mandible), soft and hard palate, as well as lips. However, we will reserve this space for discussion during the next chapter.

The Throga Technique

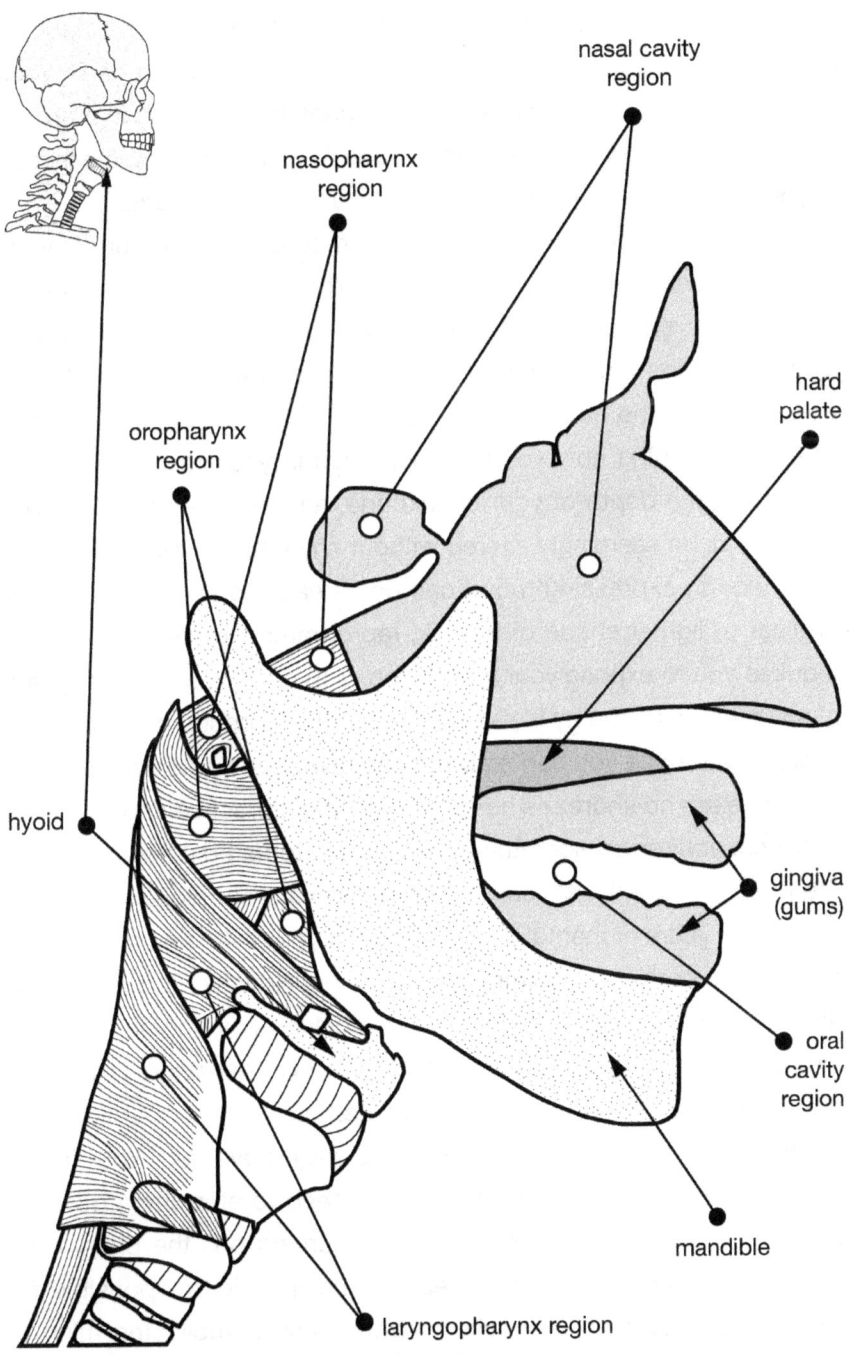

Let's use a visual analogy for altering *tone*. Think of your face, a genetic starting point for your resonating space. The shape of your eyes, the length of your nose, and the curvature of your chin are all determined by your DNA, as is the shape of your epiglottis, the length of your pharynx, and the curvature of your thyroid cartilage.

As sound waves bounce around the resonating chambers of your vocal tract, various frequencies are absorbed and reflected, resulting in a specific sound. Even the tiniest of adjustments, by dilating or lengthening the pharyngeal walls, can transform your voice. If you wear makeup, the same can be said for light as it bounces off your face, transforming how you look. The arch in your lips, the width of your eyes, the depth of your cheekbone, and even the color of your skin can all be seemingly altered without any DNA tampering.

Although expressing mood can be as easy as applying a thicker eyeliner or lighter shade of lipstick, reprogramming your core sound requires you to expose your foundation. You have to wipe away years of makeup, caked on by life's experiences. It will become much easier to work with once you can embrace the raw beauty underneath.

There are no shortcuts here. Change takes practice and patience. The more you repeat something, the more automated it becomes, and the more genetic it can *feel*. If you're 23 years old, you're going up against 23 years of mental programming. If you're 48, you're going up against 48 years of programming, and so on. However, it's mainly the first seven years of your life that you're looking to overcome, as this is when your brain defines and protects most of the behaviors you spend the rest of your life attempting to emulate.

Regardless of the behaviors that may have led you to an imbalanced or compromised sound, we need to strip them down to rebuild. You can do this by essentially "turning off" the pharyngeal walls during our practice by releasing the muscles responsible for swallowing. This may seem like a strange and complicated thing to attempt, but it's something you already know how to do. You just may not realize it yet.

Rest your fingers along the center of your throat and swallow. Did you feel your larynx slide upward? Now take a deep breath and imitate a yawn. Done correctly, you'll feel the larynx slide downward. The same muscles you use to swallow are suspending the larynx in place. So the only way for your larynx to sink down is for the muscles above, including the constrictors of the pharynx, to release. This is also why it's difficult to yawn without opening your mouth wide and surrendering your jaw muscles.

This time, try speaking your name while your larynx is down. Did you sound similar to the cartoon character Yogi Bear or Patrick from SpongeBob? So will everyone else! So much in fact, it would be difficult to tell the difference between your voice and a number of others from anywhere else in the world. By stripping away style, accent, personality, stress, and other influential behaviors that created our identifiable tone, the mask is removed and it's more reflective of our genetic starting point.

Tone Exercise
(Low larynx "Gŭ" scales)

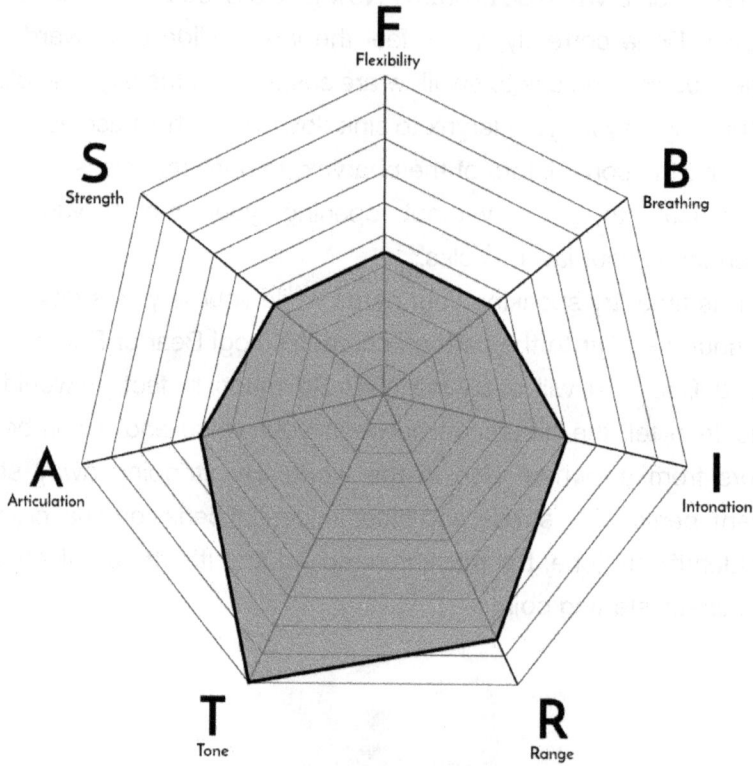

In the *Tone Exercise* (🔊 **7DS Book Media**), your goal is to remove as much behavioral makeup as possible using a "Gŭ" sound, as in the word "gum." The "G" feature, used at the beginning of each note of the one-octave scale, requires the tongue and surrounding muscles to contract upward. Your larynx should be free to move and respond naturally along with the tongue's movement. However, when sustaining a note during the "ŭ" portions of the exercise, try to encourage the larynx to rest in a lowered yawn-like position.

The Throga Technique

Given that you're seeking to improve and develop *tone*, it may seem counterintuitive to turn the muscles needed to enhance the sound into a neutral or "off" position with a lowered larynx. So to illustrate this approach, think of this repositioning as an asana for your voice. An asana, in yoga terms, refers to a sustainable position of the body. The intentional placement of the larynx, while attempting to minimize any unnecessary tensions within the vocal tract, achieves similar goals to an asana. And like many yoga positions, don't let the silliness of it throw you. The incredibly vulnerable state of a lowered larynx requires so much release, it's not uncommon for our emotional sensors to go off and start laughing as a defensive response.

The objective, of course, is not to actually sing with this strange and hollow sound for the same reasons we don't do a "downward facing dog" on the bus or at our desk while engaging with other people. Instead, various asanas are designed to help you isolate, stretch, and release both physical and mental stress, allowing you to move through your day more fluidly. Ultimately, making it easier for you to express your intentions with little to no compromise.

Don't worry if your voice sounds "good" or not, just keep your focus on form to make sure there aren't any signs of stress, especially in the shoulder or neck region. We don't want to play tug-of-war with the muscles above and below the larynx. Releasing internal stress and isolating *tone*, independent from pitches, will allow you to express the sound you choose when it comes time to sing. This is noticeably beneficial on higher notes, which require the folds to stretch more. It's also why similar exercises to this are so popular for targeting the dimension of *range*.

When vocalizing along with the practice track for *tone*, you may find that forming the "G" sound before every note causes your tongue to stiffen, making it difficult to release fully into the lowered laryngeal position. This is extremely common when first exploring this exercise, especially when it comes to the higher notes. If this is the case for you, try replacing the "G" with an "M" sound. This will allow the tongue to stay forward and relaxed while you work on the coordination of moving the larynx independently from the pitches of the scale.

Another important aspect to further develop the dimension of *tone* is to cultivate our ability to "project." Projecting frequencies within the vocal instrument should not be confused with "belting," a term often used to describe the intentional use of the chest register beyond its inherent threshold (along with a divergent shaping of the vocal tract). Projection is a more broad term, referring to vocal dynamics and volume, which relates to the resonant space of the vocal tract being in tune with the vibration of the folds. This results in a natural amplification of the sound.

Although projection is an essential skill for classical singers who must carry their voice over an orchestra without the aid of a microphone, it can be extremely beneficial to non-classical singers as well. Country, pop, gospel, rock, R&B, jazz, and metal genres all call for different tonal behaviors. But any opportunity to sing dynamically with minimal effort can truly pay off in the long run.

> *NOTE: If you chose to sing out-of-balance, be sure to maintain your instrument (stay healthy) and surround your moments of intentional imbalance, whether a single note or an entire set of songs, with as much positive behavior as possible to perform at a consistent level.*

On a related note, a common imbalance that frustrates many singers is having a "nasal" sounding voice. There are two types of nasality. First, is *hyper*-nasal, which is when too much air passes through the nasal cavities, resulting in a thin and brittle sound. Second, is *hypo*-nasal, which is when no air enters the nasal cavities, resulting in a darker, stuffy-nose, kind of sound. The soft palate, located in the upper rear of the mouth, separating the oropharynx from the nasopharynx, is mainly responsible for this air allowance.

Typically, singers only want a trace of air resonating in the nasal cavities to add some brilliance in frequency, without overpowering the overall sound. However, a touch of nasality has proven to benefit some voices and personalities in every genre. Idina Menzel, whose credits include Elphaba in *Wicked* and Elsa in *Frozen*, is a great example of this. Despite the criticism she receives for having a semi-nasally timbre, it's played a significant role in her being able to stand out and be identifiable from other skilled Broadway singers.

No matter what your goals are, maintaining a consistent quality of sound in the vocal gym is vital for long-term development. This rule applies to most exercises, regardless of the laryngeal position. Listen for tonal changes when warming up or vocalizing in general. If you catch the color of your voice changing unexpectedly, suddenly, or gradually, the muscles above your larynx may have interfered in an attempt to assist with other dimensions. The more independent *tone* becomes, the more available and intuitive your abilities will be to express the meaning of the song.

Tone Summary

- *Tone* refers to the shape or quality of sound created by the instruments' resonator (vocal tract).

- The sound you use to speak and sing is only partially determined by your DNA; most of it is learned over time.

- The quality and character of your voice are what cue emotional responses in your listeners.

- When training, learning to release the muscles above the larynx, will help make them more available for singing.

- Coordinating the muscles used for *tone* will aid in being able to project the voice.

- Having a unique or identifiable sound to your voice is usually a positive trait.

- Aim for consistency in your *tone* from lowest to highest note whenever training.

Articulation: 6th Dimension

Chapter VIII

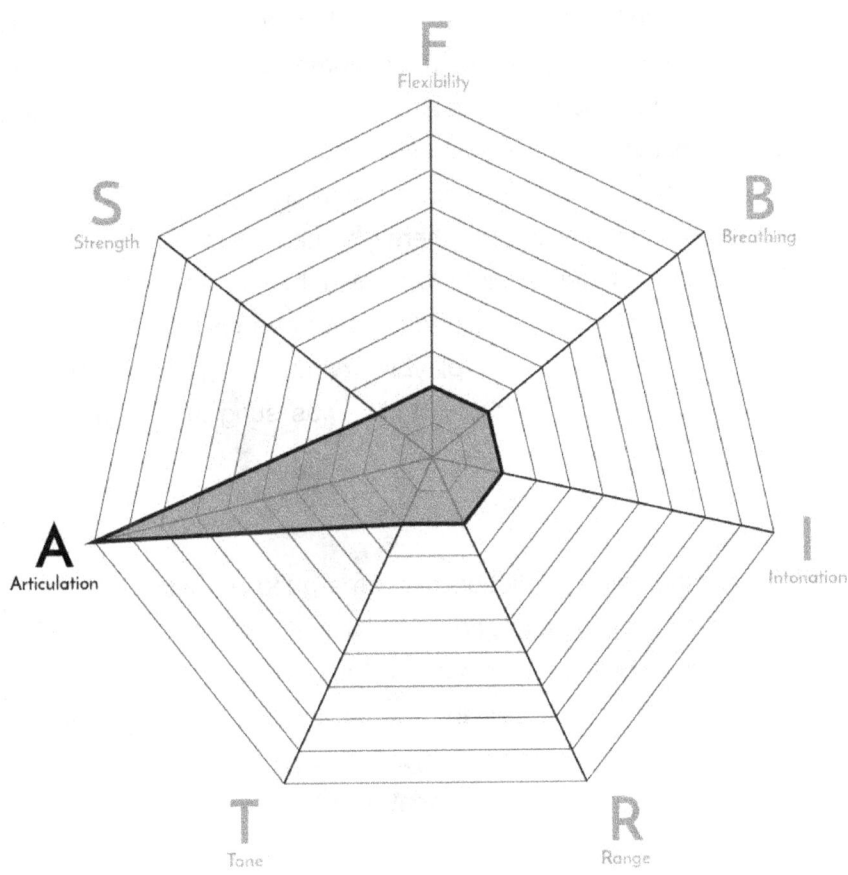

Articulation: How we pronounce words

You walk into The Royal Opera House in London for the first time. A beautiful chandelier lights the hall that greets you. As you eagerly find your seat and sit back to soak in the history behind the centuries-old design, with ornate gold leafing, a domed-shaped ceiling, and mythological carvings, the orchestra warms up and you thumb through the playbill, reading about the performers and the synopsis of the opera. Finally, the lights dim and a woman's voice cascades over the orchestra pit, consuming the hall with rich, warm overtones and a vibrato that gently pulsates your entire body. As the opening piece comes to a close, you find yourself completely immersed in the character's emotional flight, but there's something missing.

Despite nearly being brought to tears in the first ten minutes of the first act, you slowly find yourself distracted and losing interest. You scramble back through the playbill trying to figure out what's happening in the story. "I thought this was sung in English." You whisper to your neighbor.

"It is." He whispers back.

Whoops.

Though the value of diction can be argued as being artistically relative to a singer's style or genre, if a listener is distracted by having to decipher the words within a melody, they may miss the opportunity in connecting with the singer and the story being told altogether. In the above scenario, the opera singer's emotional presence was well executed, but the depth of detail that was to be laid out lyrically was lost.

This is a common occurrence, where a singer inadvertently hijacks the muscles needed for one dimension, in order to assist with another. For example, a singer's *intonation* or *tone* may be a subconscious priority over diction, which is the dimension of *articulation*. Given that muscles can only contract in one direction and stretch to a limited degree, any muscle used by one intention (or dimension) is less available for another. These imbalances are rarely by design and have a tendency to sneak up over time. Often to blame is unsupervised repetition of poor form and compromised practice when you first learn to speak and sing.

Your handwriting is formed in the same way. At first, you mimic how your parents, siblings, friends, or teachers hold a crayon. Then you trace letters and shapes to build mental programs that connect to your arms, hands, and fingers, enhancing your fine motor-skills. Over time, your body's posture and other physical behaviors, combined with your nurtured experiences of holding different shaped and weighted writing utensils on various surfaces, result in identifiable scribbles of your own. Those who are familiar with the unique patterns of your penmanship will recognize it in an instance, just as they will the unique patterns of your voice.

Inevitably, imbalances make their way into your everyday behaviors. For instance, you might have a habit of leaning heavy on your wrist as you write, risking illegibility when a surface isn't strong enough to support your arm's weight. In this analogy, think of your body's posture as the dimension of *tone* and your hand as *articulation*. The more balanced your posture is, the easier it will be to write on any surface. So the more balanced your *tone* is, the easier it will be to *articulate* any melody.

So how can you overcome these imbalances? One way is to breakdown and practice each syllable, vowel, and consonant within the melodic constructs of a song. This tedious approach would no doubt assist in the short term, one song at a time, but what about ironing out the imbalances overall? To have a truly lasting effect, the behavior needs to be addressed globally within your instrument.

Let's look again into the mechanics at play. For *articulation*, there are considerably more muscles to configure and coordinate than in any other dimension, each with their own finite contribution to bringing words into focus. To make it a bit easier to visualize, we can divide them into three distinct muscle groups:

Tongue Articulators include the tongue (superior, inferior, and transverse longitudinal) and the muscles attached to the tongue: the palatoglossus, styloglossus, hyoglossus, genioglossus, and geniohyoid.

Jaw Articulators include the mastacian and mandibular depressors: the temporalis, deep and superficial masseter, stylohyoid, digastric, mylohyoid, platysma, and pterygoid (not shown) muscles.

Lip Articulators include the orbicularis oris and the surrounding expression muscles: the levator oris and superioris, zygomaticus major and minor, depressor oris and inferioris, risorius, buccinator, and mentalis.

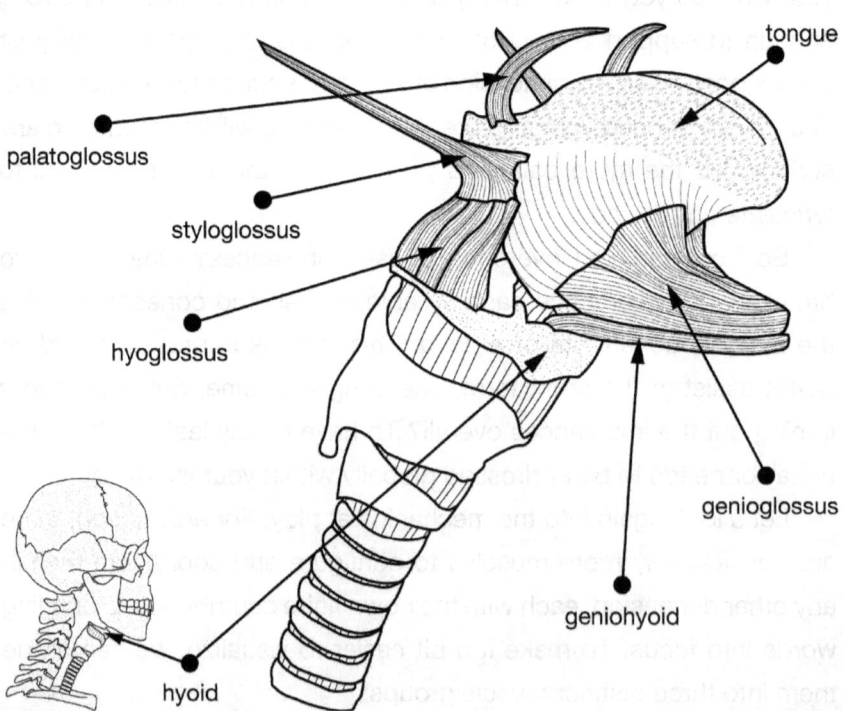

The Throga Technique

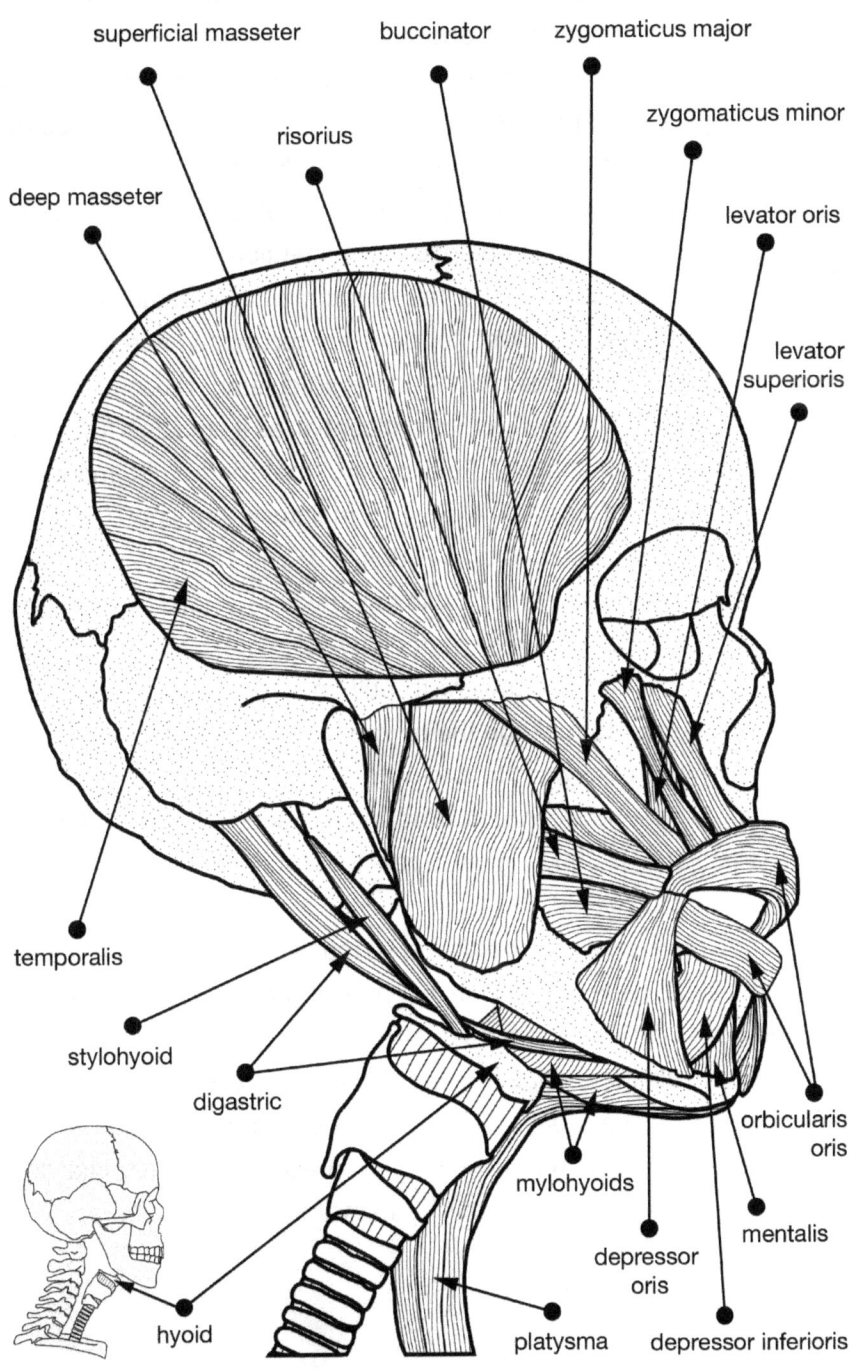

In the diagram previous to this page, notice how the larynx is suspended from the muscles above it. As the articulators move, it's natural for the larynx to "float" up and down accordingly. However, as we covered in Chapter VII, *Tone: 5th Dimension*, unnecessary involvement or stress of these muscles, including the pharyngeals not shown here, can throw your instrument out of balance, minimizing your overall ability to sing and speak with intention.

Since *articulation* shares a fair amount of real estate with the dimension of *tone*, it's best to develop as much independence between them as possible. Of the three articulatory muscle groups, the tongue's independence is most influential, as it acts as a front wall to the pharyngeal spaces. Fortunately, the tongue is made of crisscross muscle fibers, allowing it to multitask, but should still be limited to assisting *tone* and a*rticulation*.

To put this in practical terms, imagine you're singing a song and come to a part that requires the melody to decrescendo (gradually decrease in volume). If you were to pull your tongue back into your throat, in an effort to manage the air pressure by partially closing off the airway (which we want to avoid doing), you're likely to be stuck having to decide between adjusting for the sound (*tone*) or for the word (*articulation*). Juggling all three is simply too much for any sustained period of time.

A constructive way to coordinate so many muscles at once and to develop the subtleties is to "gamify" your approach. You can do this by using specific vowels (formants) and consonants (features) at a speed that rivals the tongue twisters you may have learned when you were younger. The goal will be to keep the movement of the articulatory muscles responsive and precise while maintaining independence from its overlapping dimensional neighbor, *tone*.

The Throga Technique

Articulation Exercise
(Rapid multi-formant and feature scales)

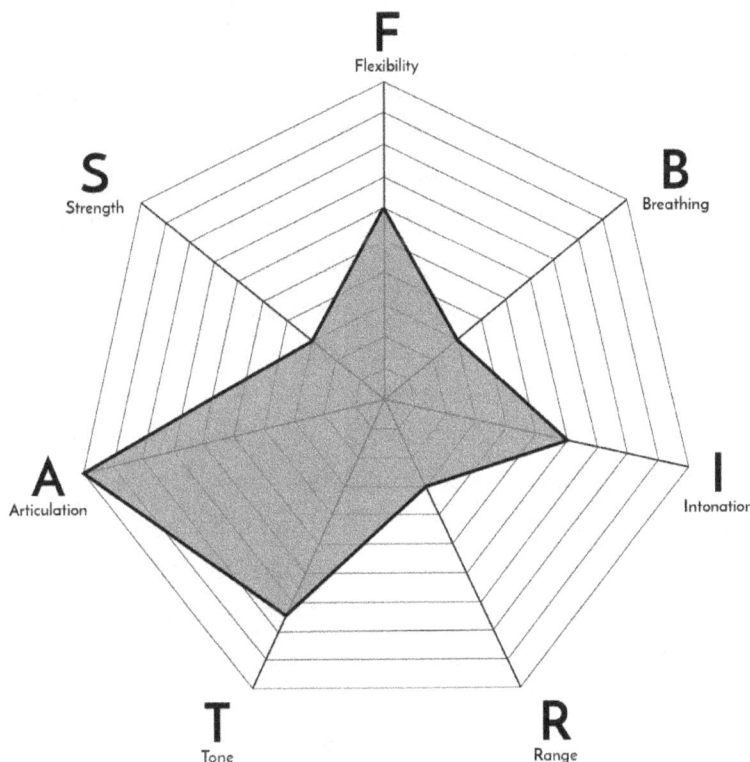

This Articulation Exercise has a lot of moving parts and easier to learn if we start with just the formants before adding in other exercise components. To begin, let's speak the five primary vowels of the standardized English alphabet out loud: a (ā), e (ē), i (ä), o (ō), u (o͞o). When pronouncing these vowels, sustain only the first part of the vowel and exclude the second vowel formation. For example, the vowel "i" is made of two formations, known as a diphthong. The first formation is an "ah" sound and the second is an "ee" sound. In this case, we only want to vocalize the "ah", which is written as "ä." To hear the correct pronunciation of each vowel, in the context of an exercise, listen to the *Articulation Exercise* "example track" in the 🔊 **7DS Book Media** or reference the pronunciation key in Chapter XII, *Vocal-Exercise Mapping*. Now try saying them forward and back in this order several times: ā, ē, ä, ō, o͞o, ō, ä, ē, ā.

Next, let's add a feature before each of the formants, or vowels, using other letters of the alphabet. Start with a "B" by repeating Bā, Bē, Bä, Bō, Bo͞o, Bō, Bä, Bē, Bā as fast as you can. The goal is not to lose any audible clarity of either the B feature or the formant. It's tricky at first, but once you have it down, you can apply this to a simple five-note pattern on a major scale. The *Articulation Exercise* loops this scale twice, first giving you a chance to practice the coordination at a slower pace before doubling in speed.

After successfully vocalizing the "B" with clarity, start moving through other available features: D, F, G, H, J, K, L, M, N, P, Q, R, S, T, V, W, X, Y, Z, CH, SH, TH, and NG. Each will present its own little challenges, some more significant than others. Exploring every feature will touch upon all 120 primary vowel and consonant combinations in the English language. That's no small feat, but well worth the effort since you'll be using them for the rest of your life.

If you sing in other languages, consider changing out the features to reflect those languages. If you sing in Hawaiian, for example, you can practice the consonants used in the Hawaiian alphabet: H, K, L, M, N, P, and W with the same five formants. This way, you can take on a variety of feature and formant combinations while directly developing the consonants and vowels you use to sing.

> NOTE: Using a mirror to monitor your facial and neck movements will also provide more feedback to assist in maximizing the benefits of this exercise.

The Throga Technique

When you're ready to advance, try combining and alternating features. The more similar they are to each other, the more difficult it will be. For example: B/P (Bā, Pē, Bä, Pō, Bōō, Pō, Bä, Pē, Bā) to target your lips, D/T (Dā, Tē, Dä, Tō, Dōō, Tō, Dä, Tē, Dā) to target the tip of the tongue, and G/K (Gā, Kē, Gä, Kō, Gōō, Kō, Gä, Kē, Gā) to target the rear of the tongue.

You can raise your volume as well, but make sure you maintain good form. Returning to our previous analogy to handwriting, getting loud without regard to form would be like pressing down hard as you try to write without regard to the surface you're writing on. Your agenda to elicit emotion may be expressed well, but you risk losing another layer of clarity. For instance, your peripheral vision has already cued your brain that something exciting or important is about to be expressed to you, because this paragraph ends with ALL CAPITAL LETTERS!!!!! AND A COMPLETE DISREGARD TO THE AMOUNT OF "!!!!" AFTER IT!!!!

Notice the tone of voice in the above example, though internalized, was processed by your mind emotionally before you interpreted the letters into words and articulated their meaning. This is just like your opera experience earlier, where your mind triggered emotional responses, before realizing something was missing.

Of all the dimensions, this is perhaps the most obvious one to develop and connect directly to singing. After all, you hardly need an expert to tell you if your words are clear. Nonetheless, recording and listening back to yourself may reveal some subtle imbalances you may have missed during practice. The independence of the muscles related to *articulation* are easy to be taken for granted, as they're so easy to rely on in a last moment plea to fix the imbalance of other dimensions of the voice.

Articulation Summary

- *Articulation* refers to the coordination and independence of the muscles used for diction.

- Often sacrificed when singing, this dimension adds another layer of storytelling and emotional depth.

- The muscles related to *articulation* can be broken into three groups: tongue, jaw, and lips.

- *Articulation* shares real estate with the dimension of *tone*, but focuses on the refinement of the core sound.

- Developing independence between the muscles for phonating and the muscles for *articulation* is key to improving diction.

- Quick paced exercises that utilize multiple formants and/or multiple features (from any language) will help target *articulation*.

Strength: 7th Dimension

Chapter IX

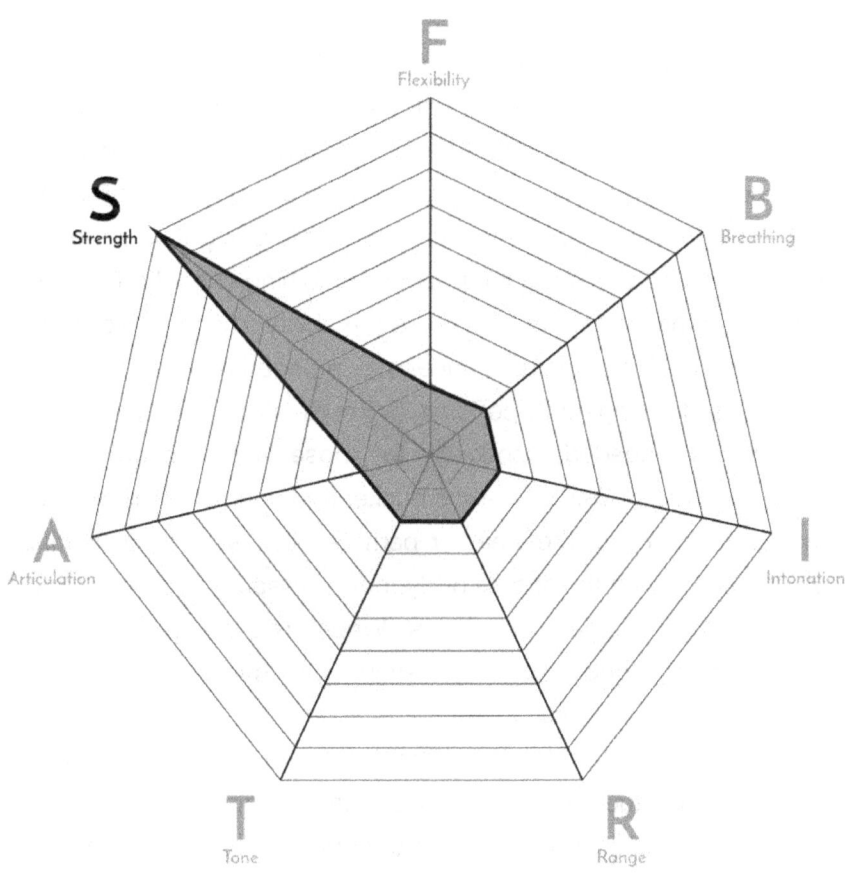

Strength: The stability and stamina of the voice

Earlier we talked about the dimension of *range*, represented by the speed of a bike and our ability to shift gears smoothly. *Strength*, our final dimension, would be like controlling the speed while pedaling up and down varying degrees of incline, and for great distances. Having an efficient balance of minimal tension and pressure in each moment, no matter how rough the terrain, is what allows an experienced cyclist to pedal for hours with a sense of ease and consistency.

When referring to vocal strength, it should not be perceived as a mere measurement of power. After all, using a "strong" color on your lips, such as bright orange, requires no more physical effort than applying a "weaker" hue, such as pale beige. Being loud or forceful does not accurately account for our ability to sing strongly. True vocal strength, in the context of singing, is the ability to convey your vocal intentions, relative to circumstance, over a period of time.

In order for singers to perform for hours, stamina and stability of the voice are needed, especially for those who depend on their musical earnings. Alex, a full-time busker and songwriter, is one such individual. Whenever the weather permits, Alex will sing an endless set of songs out on the streets of Sydney, massaging the wrinkles out of his voice, melodies, and lyrics. When he's not gigging in the elements or at a pub late into the evening, he's in the studio writing and tracking new material.

Alex's commitment to his craft and ability to sustain it vocally was carved out over the years. Part of his training regimen circled around *flexibility*, to minimize fatigue, and *strength*, to support a career of singing day after day, traveling from country to country. It's also what helped prepare his instrument to survive the pressures related to being on live TV, in front of millions of viewers, making it all the way to the finals on *The Voice*.

The Throga Technique

* top view of larynx

- hyoid
- vocal fold
- thyroid cartilage
- thyroarytenoid
- vocalis
- lateral cricoarytenoid
- posterior cricoarytenoid
- transverse arytenoid
- oblique arytenoid
- cricothyroid

Mechanically, the *7 Dimensions of Singing* describes *strength* as the collective coordination, capacity, and stability of the intrinsic laryngeal muscles. This includes the thyroarytenoid (vocalis), cricothyroid, and the arytenoid muscles responsible for adduction (bringing the folds together) as well as abduction (the separation of the folds).

These muscles consist of two types of muscle fibers; slow-twitch fibers, measured by endurance, and fast-twitch fibers, measured by force. One way to address all of these muscles simultaneously is with volume swells, isolating one pitch at a time, as in the following Strength Exercise.

Strength Exercise
(Counting swells on single notes)

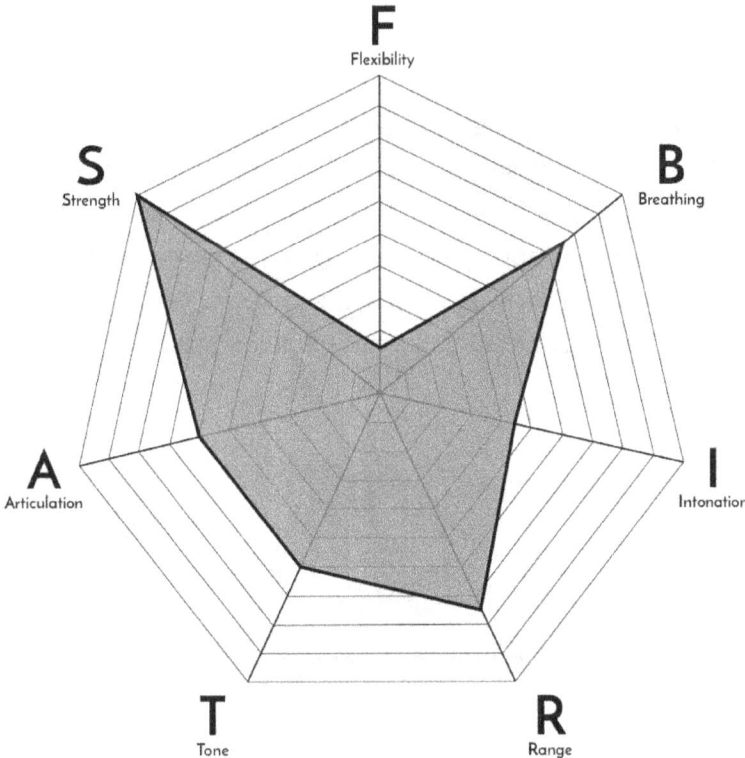

Vocalizing on a single pitch, without having to adjust to multiple speeds of vibration, helps us hone in on the dimension of *strength*. To optimize the simplicity of this one-note pattern, we can deliberately modify the volume, or decibel level, by increasing and decreasing the subglottic pressure. This is a unique approach compared to most exercises, in which we strive to keep the volume steady. However, we still need to follow the guideline of maintaining intentional volumes throughout.

7 Dimensions of Singing

For this exercise, we're going to use numbers, counting from one to five and back down again, to divide the relative volumes as demonstrated on *strength*'s "example track" in the 🔊 **7DS Book Media**. Volume "1" should be as quiet as you can be while maintaining a clear tone. Volume "2" will be slightly louder than volume "1", volume "3" even louder, and so on. On volume "5," when you're as loud as you be without any signs of struggle, make sure to maintain good form. Meaning, don't sacrifice any of the Throga Guidelines just to keep the note steady.

The following graph depicts our goal, which is to delineate an audible distinction between each number, as well as match the volumes on the way up with the ones coming back down:

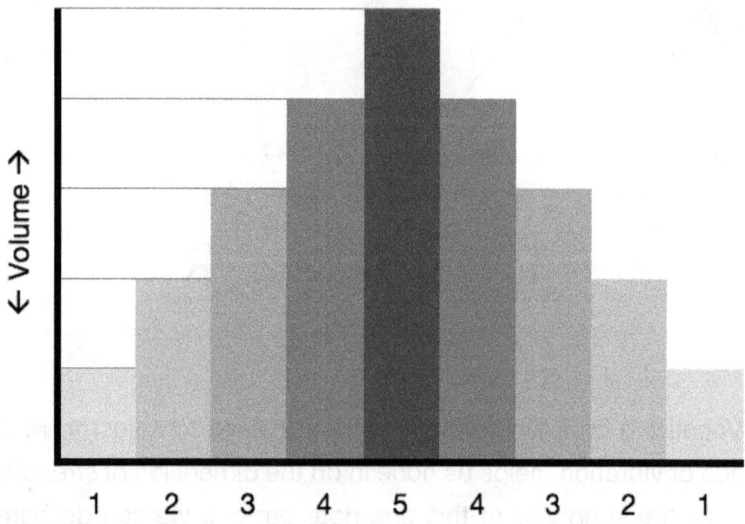

As you will soon discover, every note you explore will result in a different measurement of decibels. While volume "1" will remain constant from your lowest to highest note, volumes "2" through "5"

will expand relative to the frequency, acoustical space, and the amount of air pressure applied.

This exercise becomes particularly challenging in the area of notes where volume "1" is in your head register with the folds in a thinner position than when vocalizing volume "5," somewhere in your chest register. In the same way that glissando patterns can target the passaggio by sliding up and down notes on a steady *volume*, a simple pattern can do so by sliding up and down volume on a steady *note*.

Now, so long as you're hydrated and have already taken the time to warm up, try vocalizing with the *Strength Exercise* "practice track" in the 🔊 **7DS Book Media**. As you can see by the 7DS graph of this exercise, highlighting the targeted dimensions, there's a lot to juggle. But there's no questioning the value in gaining control over your volume, independent of your pitches. Imagine the freedom of expression that coincides with being able to sing any note, on any vowel, at any volume.

When you're ready to dig in deeper and optimize the level of difficulty that volume-swell exercises can offer, try replacing the numbers with a steady "ä" formant. By removing the features that are built into the numbers, such as the "N" in the word "one" and the "T" in "two", more breath control and stability of the folds will be required. In addition to the change in formant, you can do a gradual increase and decrease of volume. This is known as a crescendo and decrescendo, where the volume adjusts smoothly rather than jumping from one decibel to another. This modification will boost the development of the dimension of *range* as well.

This variation is like learning to smoothly shift into lower gears on your bike while pedaling uphill, and then shifting into higher ones just as smoothly on the way back down instead of coasting and wearing out the hand brakes. A volume graph for this alternative version looks like this:

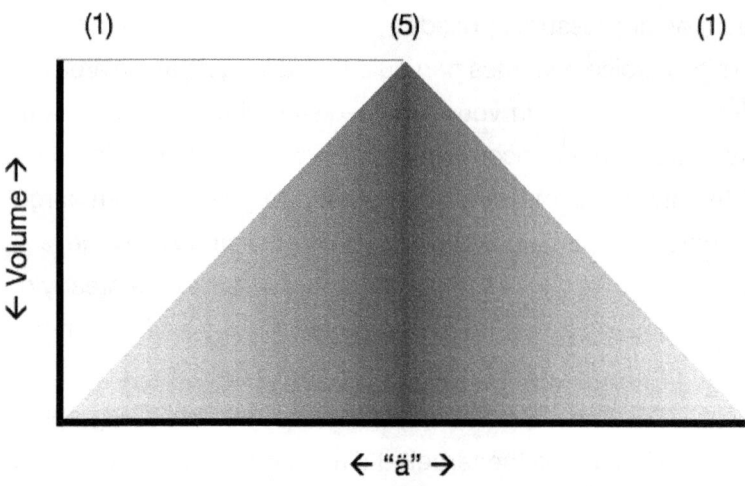

To illustrate this point about every pitch having access to different levels of volume, let's try a quick experiment. Imagine Alex is standing far away from you. He's busking on the other side of the street, and you want to gain his attention by shouting his name. Instead of blurting it out at some random frequency, take a moment to find your lowest possible speaking note.

Got it?

Now try shouting "Alex!" on that same pitch.

Not so easy, is it?

The reason we intuitively increase our pitch when aiming for louder volumes is that frequencies can only be amplified in a space large enough for them to do so. Low frequencies especially need adequate room for them to expand for the complete sound wave to be heard correctly. This is why instruments that produce low notes like tubas and cellos have larger resonators than higher note-producing instruments like trumpets and violins.

Regrettably, *strength* is a dimension that many singers skip in their training. That is until they're in a "trial by fire" situation! This could be when getting the lead in a high school musical, performing seven nights a week on a cruise ship, maybe recording a full-length album, or being featured on network TV. Those who neglect this dimension, intentionally or not, have a tendency to get sick, fatigue quickly, and break down emotionally. This can lead to highly inconsistent performances and even lose the opportunity at hand all together.

To sum up, a strong voice is a consistent voice. With a little balance, momentum, and the willingness to practice, singing can be as easy as riding a bike. If you want to cycle in rough weather, up the side of a mountain, or achieve really long distances, balancing all seven dimensions will carry you all the way to the finish line.

Strength Summary

- *Strength* refers to the overall stability and stamina of the intrinsic muscles of the larynx.

- Don't think of *strength* as a measurement of vocal power or force. More so, a measurement of consistency in executing your vocal intentions under any circumstance.

- Single notes target *strength* because they don't require the folds to continuously stretch to varying degrees.

- Intentionally modifying volume throughout your range will challenge and develop *strength*.

- Lower notes are harder to project than higher notes because they require a larger resonator (vocal tract).

- Singers often neglect developing vocal *strength* until opportunity knocks, which can be costly. So don't wait to start developing it.

7DS on Stage

Chapter X

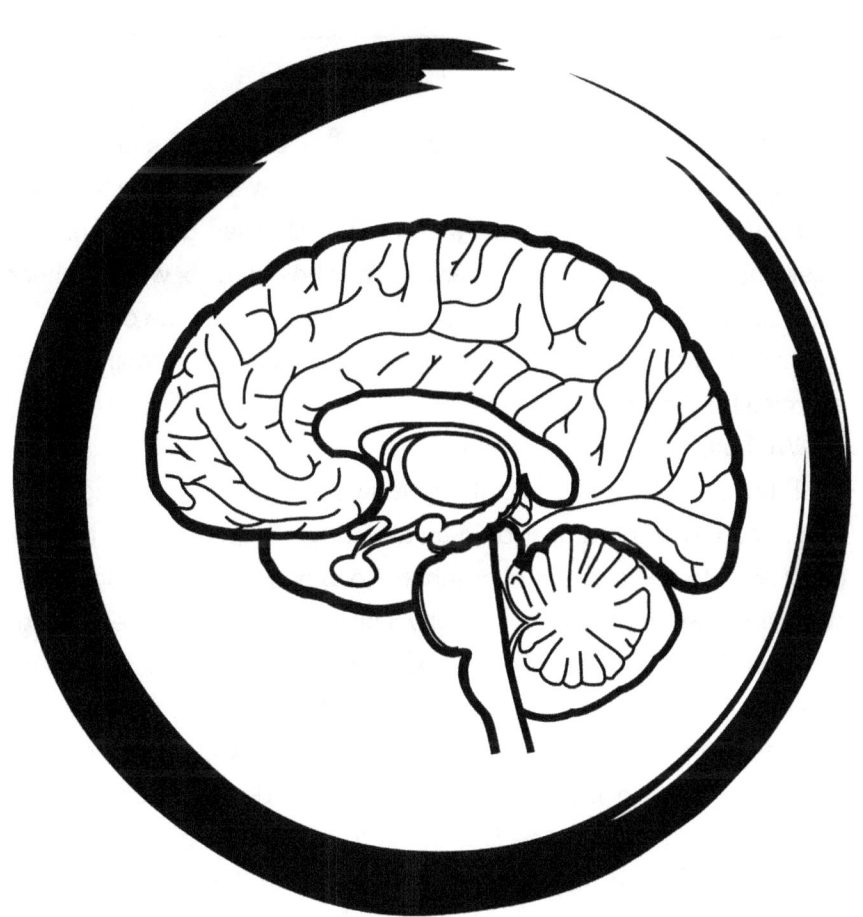

"All the world's a stage, and all the men and women merely players."

- William Shakespeare (1564 - 1616)

Now that we've analyzed each of the dimensions under the spotlight, it's time we take a step back to see how they come together collectively in the limelight. As we learned, all seven dimensions co-exist whenever we phonate, regardless of where we are, who can hear us, or what the sound may be. So how do we separate the concept of the vocal gym from the stage? Practice from performance? Or exercise from art?

With only a thought.

If the vocal gym is only a thought away, so can be the stage. We don't need to be on a riser or in an auditorium to perform, just as we don't need to be holding a microphone to experience stage fright. The stage, like the vocal gym, has no physical address. It's a state of mind.

Over the years, there've been several insightful studies done on music's interactivity with the brain using fMRI (functional magnetic resonance imaging) machines. These neuroimaging machines use MRI technology to measure brain activity by detecting changes in blood flow. When someone first learns to play a new piece of music, the fMRI shows the prefrontal cortex, located in the front part of the brain, illuminating brightly as he or she consciously processes and calculates what to do. This reflects the activity of being in the vocal gym.

In one particular study, a highly skilled jazz pianist was monitored while improvising a melody on a special. Here, the results showed that the prefrontal cortex, normally allocated for planning, self-consciousness, and rationalization, dimmed greatly. However, other areas of the brain associated with emotions, motivation, long-term memory, and fine motor skills lit up like a firework show. This reflects the activity of being on stage.

You see, without having to succumb to worry and social acceptance, musicians (including singers) can express themselves unrestrictedly and play by "feel" when interpreting a song. After all, the last thing you want to be thinking about in a performance is the position of your larynx, the tension of the vocal folds, or how much air you might need for the line to come.

In the next section, *Mindful Singing*, we'll dive a little deeper into the rabbit hole that is the singer's brain. There, we're going to discover that if we change our *thinking*, we can actually change our *singing*.

Mindful Singing

The subconscious mind, distributed in several areas of the brain, is a database of personal experiences and programs that can process millions of bits of information simultaneously with flawless execution. You draw from these programs in order to function in everyday life, including the actions and processes related to singing. The conscious mind (prefrontal cortex), on the other hand, is only capable of juggling a handful of things at once, and not always successfully.

The reason for this is simple; the subconscious cannot make rational decisions or contemplate moral dilemmas. It can't see the difference between what's good from bad or what's right from wrong. It can only take information in, store it, and play it back. In other words, there is no filtering system that would otherwise slow it down or potentially create errors. These programs are what drive our actions, which we refer to as skills.

Since you, your conscious self is unable to consult with your subconscious, the programs you've cultivated and stored for speaking and singing will run your behaviors automatically. Just as your programs do for kicking a ball, riding a bicycle, or writing your name down. The challenge here is that you can only be aware of so much at a time. So if it weren't for the amazing replay skills of the subconscious, you would barely be able to open your mouth and moan, let alone say a complete sentence or hum a melody. The question then is, "How does a singer with flawed behavior being played back by the subconscious, change her programming in order to sing better?"

You are already aware of the answer of course. It's been suggested to you time and time again since you were a child, and even more recently throughout this book. The answer is "practice." This may seem oversimplified and obvious, but consciously repeating a new behavior will literally rewrite the stored programs in your subconscious, no matter how complex or ingrained they may be. The power of mindful repetition will rewrite your history, your beliefs, and ultimately, your voice.

For professional singers, well-balanced skills are necessary to sustain a career. Unfortunately, there is no shortage of unexpected and often unfavorable circumstances in which a singer has to depend solely on their subconscious and how deeply it's programmed. Katy Perry had to fight off tears upon receiving news of her divorce, just moments before stepping on stage during her *California Dreams* tour. Luciano Pavarotti sang in Baja, California in front of 35,000 people in the midst of a high-fevered flu. The Beatles performed at Shea Stadium in 1965 with no means to hear themselves over the screaming fans. It was through countless hours of practice and balanced behavior that allowed these singers to meet, and even exceed their audience's expectation, despite the emotional, physical, or technical disturbances the singer had to endure.

There's no doubt that building positive behaviors will allow you to run your mechanical needs on autopilot. However, the condition and health of your mind and body will significantly influence your performance. How you live your life, what you eat, how you sleep, how you talk, and how you think of yourself all factor in. For example, if you don't consume the proper nutrition, your body can start to malfunction, causing a negative domino effect on your immune system, hydration levels, muscle tissue, and so on.

In the same respect, if you think of yourself as a bad singer (conscious mind), then that too will cause a negative ripple effect in your body, causing tension and mismanagement of your instrument's behaviors. If you repeat the belief or thought of having an incapacity to sing often enough, your subconscious will then write programs to support it, making it even more difficult to achieve whatever vocal aspirations you may have.

Remember, your subconscious isn't doing anything wrong here. It's simply playing back what you downloaded to it. If you don't like the programs being played, then you need to download new information. This way, what is seemingly "normal" or "natural" right now, can shift into a new feeling of familiarity and comfort. Then you will no longer be under the hypnotic illusion of being born a bad singer or a victim of genetic circumstance.

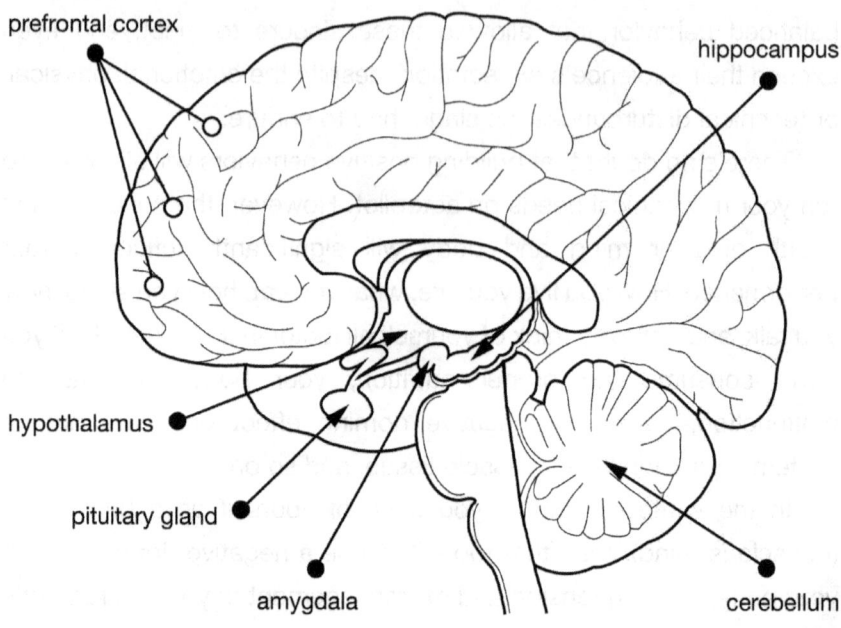

Singing, not so surprisingly, requires more parts of your brain than any other physical activity. A harmony of mindful intention and subconscious programming is needed to vocalize in the vocal gym. And though this may be technically enough to get through a song, it is the influence of your emotions, stemming from the limbic system and the *un*conscious mind, that brings a song to life.

The limbic system manages your pre-rational programming (your unconsciousness), which consists of emotional, regulatory, and protective operations. The structures of the brain associated with these functions include the hypothalamus, which regulates hormone production via the pituitary gland and things like thirst, breathing, mood, response to pain and pleasure, and circadian rhythm. Next we have the hippocampus, which converts short-term memory into long-term memory. And finally, the amygdala and several other nearby areas, regulate a variety of emotions along with our "fight or flight" response. Collectively, they can release a cocktail of reflex instructions to the body, rich with endorphins and chemicals such as adrenaline, oxytocin, and dopamine, in response to singing and how you perceive your immediate surroundings.

In order to take advantage of what this system has to offer in your artistic expression, you must gate your unconsciousness with the right balance of vulnerability. Since the unconscious mind receives and filters all incoming information before the conscious mind can review it, its programmed reflex signals can have an overwhelming impact on your voice, especially when singing. If the signals are too strong, you will lose control over your breathing, pitches, and so forth. Adversely, if you overly censor the information received, then your performance can seem disconnected and underwhelming.

Fortunately, your unconsciousness and its seemingly impenetrable, hard-wired, pre-programmed abilities are also vulnerable to change. In fact, mindful meditation has been used to override unconscious programming for ages. Yogi masters do it to take control of their autonomic body functions for self-healing and to pursue a "higher state of consciousness." Method actors do it to train their body's reactions to reflect the character's traits rather than their own. Free divers do it to lower their heart rate and body temperature to minimize oxygen usage when diving. Of course, you don't need to be able to hold your breath under water for ten minutes in order to sing a song. You just need to dim the lights in your prefrontal cortex so you can sit back and enjoy the fireworks.

But how can we do this? How can we create a harmonious relationship between the conscious, subconscious, and unconscious minds while simultaneously singing a song? The answer is much less complex than one might expect; we let the lyrics guide us.

Think of the lyrics in a song as a form of guided meditation. Guided meditation is when an instructor walks a listener through different points of self-awareness, one step at a time. Imagery and various forms of movement are often used as a means to quiet the consciousness and enliven other aspects of the mind. Lyrics offer us the same opportunity. They invite the singer to react to the connotation of the words being sung by tapping into their own life experiences and programming.

To better facilitate this concept, let's try an experiment. Select a song you'd like to work on and print out the lyrics with enough space to write above each line. Next, read each line while considering the mood of the melody and song to interpret the emotion(s) you feel should be portrayed. Then write those emotions above the relevant lyrics throughout the entire piece. Some songs might just repeat the word "happy," whereas other songs might morph from happy, to hopeful, to longing, to desperate, and back to happy again, in the first verse alone. In the end, you'll see how this handwritten, meditative guide can transform words into meaning, beyond simply mimicking someone else's interpretation of a song.

Each new song will be a different voice leading you down a different path. If you yield to their directional whispers, they will poke and prod at a wide array of emotional activity within you, allowing you to merge a barrage of subconscious and innate responses. These responses will produce unique adjustments in your breathing, your volume, your tone, and your pitch. As well as muscular tensions and releases throughout your body and throughout your singing, just as you do when speaking "from the heart." The more honest and authentic your delivery is, the more likely your audience will be able to experience a shared unconsciousness, exponentially amplifying the emotional intent of the song.

"People will forget what you said, people will forget what you did, but people will never forget how you made them feel."

- Maya Angelou (1928 - 2014)

It's in our human nature to want to feel good about ourselves and to seek others who feel and think similarly as we do. If we can trigger joy, awe, or familiarity within someone else's programming, as Maya suggests, then they will attach us, our voices, and that feeling, converting a short-term memory into a long-term memory. From being an admirer for a moment, into being a fan for life.

7DS On Stage Summary

- The stage is not a physical location; it is a state of mind, like the vocal gym.

- You use a combination of your conscious, subconscious, and unconscious to sing and vocalize.

- The conscious mind is your self-awareness and planning, the subconscious mind is a database of stored information and learned behaviors, and the unconscious mind refers to your emotional and fight or flight responses.

- Repetition of a thought or action rewrites subconscious programming over time.

- Vulnerability is essential in expressing yourself and connecting with others.

- Lyrics can be used as a singer's guide to accurately express the song's emotional intent.

Diagnostics and Solutions

Chapter XI

Now that we've discussed each of the 7 Dimensions of Singing, are you ready to unveil which dimensions you need to develop in order to skillfully express your emotional intentions? For this, we need to step out of the vocal gym and onto the stage. Yes, you finally get to sing something, where the rules outlined by the *Throga Guidelines* no longer apply.

First, find a place as private as possible, such as your bedroom or vehicle, to minimize any self-conscious disruptions. Next, select a song whose lyrics you know very well, so you can sing it a capella (no musical background) with your eyes closed, and focus on its meaning. It can be something you wrote, a popular song you can cover, an aria, a hymn, or even a nursery rhyme. Just choose something you know, regardless of how well you think you might do.

Did you select one?

Go ahead and sing it.

How did it feel? Did you use the lyrics as an emotional guide? Were there any restrictions or limitations in your ability to express the song the way you imagined it? If so, the following diagnostics guide will help reveal which dimension(s) may have been out of balance:

Do FLEXIBILITY exercises IF:
- the quality of your voice sounds worn or fatigued
- your voice isn't responding quickly to your intentions
- your voice is cracking in the passaggio unusually often

Do BREATHING exercises IF:
- you struggle to sustain long notes or phrases
- you feel the need to inhale in awkward parts of the song
- you sound unintentionally airy or breathy

The Throga Technique

Do INTONATION exercises IF:
- you're not able to match your intended pitches
- you unintentionally slide in or out of the notes
- you struggle to remember the melody or harmony

Do RANGE exercises IF:
- your voice cracks between registers at various volumes
- you feel and/or hear strain on higher notes
- you're unable to sing the lowest or highest note in the song

Do TONE exercises IF:
- the sound of your voice doesn't match what you intended
- your quality of sound is inconsistent throughout the song
- the sound of your voice is generally unpleasing to your ears

Do ARTICULATION exercises IF:
- the words you're singing aren't clear to understand
- you feel tension in your tongue, jaw, or lip regions
- you unintentionally modify the vowels (formants)

Do STRENGTH exercises IF:
- you struggle to increase or decrease volume when desired
- your voice sounds generally unstable or inconsistent
- you notice signs of fatigue even after warming up

Now that you know how to relate the symptom to its connected dimension, try singing the same song again. This time, record your performance on a phone or tablet and listen back to it for better objectivity. Keep in mind, we're not aiming to change how we sing during this diagnostic exercise. We are only observing.

As you can see, putting just one song under the 7-dimensional spotlight will help eliminate how these imbalances will affect how we sing now and in future performances too.

On and Off Stage Solutions

The best singing comes when you're able to successfully apply your programmed skills and interpret the song with emotional, rather than mechanical, intentions. Allowing the nuance of your natural tendencies and personality traits to seep into your vocal style and delivery can prevent a stiff or manufactured sound. For example, if Adele were to cover a song originally performed by Rihanna, she wouldn't even consider mimicking Rihanna's vocal style or tonal delivery and would more than likely change the song's key and production together. If she were to mimic her, it would create confusion in the minds of Adele's listeners as to who she is as an artist and potentially risk an emotional detachment between her and her fans.

In another scenario, you may be acting out a character, such as Jean Valjean or Fantine in the musical, *Les Misérables*. Here, your director or producer might have you perform with an accent or move with an unusual posture that is not genuinely your own. Bending the authenticity of who you are as an individual doesn't mean you can't still connect with the role's emotional intent. It's a matter of allowing the limbic system to flourish while still being consciously present in the scripted guides of the song and character.

Regardless of genre or character related restrictions, if you're unable to express the lyrics and melody as you imagine them (or are expected to), you can apply your knowledge of the seven dimensions directly to the songs you're working on, either *on* or *off* stage. Targeting a dimension *on* stage refers to short-term adjustments of the song's parameters or within your vocal delivery. These are TEMPORARY solutions in an effort to sing as dynamically and cleverly as possible, under the present conditions and available programming.

Targeting a dimension *off* stage refers to bringing the melody of the song into the vocal gym by replacing the lyrics, and therefore the emotional triggers, with a relevant exercise. Removing the lyrics will not only desensitize the melody to reveal its musical bones; it will light the prefrontal cortex back up with a spotlight on details such as pitch, volume, and formant for a more globalized development, benefiting your long-term goals and future performances.

Try applying both the on and off stage solutions below for each of the dimensions you wish to improve upon. Ideally, you'll only have to use a single suggested solution to make a significant contribution toward your performance. However, be sure to remove any on stage solutions from your practice as soon as you're able, so you can continue to grow. Many of these suggestions benefit multiple dimensions, not just the one it may be listed under. For this reason, they have been categorized relative to the dimension it will benefit the most, but not in a particular order:

Flexibility Solutions

ON STAGE: If you believe *flexibility* to be an issue, the first thing to address is the general health of your instrument: if you are sleep deprived, take a nap; if you are dehydrated, drink water; if you haven't warmed-up yet, do so. That being said, here are a few things you can do to accommodate your current condition and available skills for an immediate performance:

- Keep your body in motion to help neutralize general tensions, even if standing in one area behind a microphone.

- Do simple *flexibility* orientated exercises to stretch the vocal folds in between songs and during instrumental parts away from the microphone.

- Temporarily close the vowel shapes (formants) slightly in order to create more backpressure, allowing the folds to become more responsive.

- If possible, lower the key of the song to make the higher notes more accessible. This may also require additional modifications of the melody on lower notes.

OFF STAGE: We can target dimensions within a specific song using lyric-replacement exercises. For flexibility, bring the melody of the song you want to work with into the vocal gym by following its notational patterns and phrasing in place of a traditional scale. Here, we will apply the *Throga Guidelines* to target *flexibility* with a lip-trill rather than lyrics. A lip-trill is a "brrrr" sound you might use to imitate a pretend car or boat. The closure of the lips against the air being released provides a lot of backpressure, making it easy for the vocal folds to stretch and vibrate quickly. If you're unable to do a lip-trill, try a tongue roll or a simple "m" formant.

Breathing Solutions

ON STAGE: Mismanagement of airflow is a common culprit for poor vocal performances. However, if you notice the dimension of *breathing* only appears to be out of balance when singing in front of others, you're likely to be experiencing a form of performance-related anxiety. Stress in the mind will manifest itself in the body, oftentimes disrupting the natural flow of breathing. Basic meditational exercises leading up to performances are a great way to help relax the mind. But once you're on stage, whether or not you feel nervous, try one or more of these temporary solutions to regain your balance for *breathing*:

- Consciously inhale through your nose, whenever the spacing of a melody permits, to help calm the mind and keep the diaphragm actively engaged.

- Sing with a clear tone, whenever appropriate, in order to avoid airy or imbalanced sounds that may require additional air.

- If you're highly active on stage, reduce your body's movement to help reserve oxygen usage, but avoid standing totally still, which can lead to stiffening.

- When permitted, adjust the tempo in order to assist in the pacing of your breath: speed up if struggling with long slow legato melodies, or slow down if you're unable to catch your breath during quick-paced phrasing.

OFF STAGE: In this lyric replacement exercise, we can borrow directly from Chapter IV, *Breathing: 2nd Dimension*, by replacing the syllables of each word and note change with a "Hē." The challenge is to maintain a consistent volume, quality, and duration of each "H" from the beginning to the end of the phrase. Do your best to inhale only in the spaces you would normally when singing the song. You can also modify the degree of difficulty by raising or lowering the overall volume.

Intonation Solutions

ON STAGE: If you're reliant on being able to hear yourself well in order to sing in tune, you'll have many frustrating performances to come. The reason for this is that stage environments are rarely as accommodating as you may be used to in rehearsals or when singing by yourself. Granted, an acoustically balanced setting is ideal, but being heavily dependent on stage monitors or in-ears means you are continuously responding to what *was*, a millisecond in the past, rather than to what *is* in the moment. It takes time to develop this sense of trust within your instrument. In the meantime, try these on stage solutions:

- Simplify the melody or riff if the melodic intervals are too complicated or result in undefined note selections.

- Adjust the stylization of the song to intentionally slide or bend into notes when and wherever appropriate.

- Wear a single earplug or adjust the monitors so that you can hear the notes you're singing more clearly.

- Introduce or invite additional vibrato to help reduce tension and mask off-pitch moments within the melody.

OFF STAGE: For relatively slow songs, try replacing the words with the "z-pulse" technique discussed in Chapter V, *Intonation: 3rd Dimension*. For up-tempo songs, apply a legato "z" formant, stringing the notes of the melody together without sliding from one to the other. Once again, be sure to teleport back to the vocal gym mindset during this process and remove any emotional aspects of your delivery. This way, you can practice a more accurate approach to executing the pitches by re-writing subconscious programs in your singing.

Range Solutions

ON STAGE: Firstly, don't be afraid to adapt a melody or key of a song to accommodate your voice. This may not always be possible when fulfilling character expectations, such as singing a role in a musical. However, a "high" note is only relative to the inhabiting "low" note within a piece of music. For example, if you were to sing only above a C5 for an entire song, the audience would quickly become numb to the notion that you were singing high notes at all. Yet, if you sang two octaves under that for the first half of the song and then only went up to a C4 in the bridge, the contrast would grab the audience's full attention by appearing as high. This is similar to waking up at two in the morning and being blinded by the same bathroom light, that is barely bright enough for you to read the shampoo label during the day. The power of relativity is an essential tool in delivering a dynamic and memorable performance, regardless of whatever range of notes may be currently accessible. Try these short-term solutions to take advantage of where you are with the song at hand:

- Increase or decrease the volume, or air pressure, in order to strategically place notes around the passaggio and allow for the voice to "crack" between registers when and where appropriate.

- Consciously reduce neck tension and avoid looking or reaching upward in association with a high note, which tends to invite more effort than necessary.

- Change only the notes of the melody you are struggling with, whether low or high

- If circumstances allow, adjust the entire key of the song up or down to make the notes of the melody more accessible.

OFF STAGE: Here, we can work to increase *range* for performances further down the road by taking advantage of the lower laryngeal position as described in the *tone* exercise. In this scenario, we want to do a "MŭM" lyrical replacement with a lowered posture of the larynx throughout the entire melody. The "M" combined with the "ŭ" formant is selected to make it easier to access higher notes and steer through the passaggio. This will provide a model of minimal tension in which we want to ultimately be able to sing. As a reminder, our objective of the lowered larynx is to reduce unwanted tension and not to mimic the tone of the exercise in the context of a song.

Tone Solutions

ON STAGE: Since your audience will intuitively respond to your *tone* before processing what's actually being said, it's best to sing as authentically as possible by being connected to the emotional guide of the lyrics. If you're struggling to make this connection, try applying these on stage solutions:

- Exaggerate the emotional intent of the lyrics to make the general delivery of the song more dynamic.

- Deliberately modify your tonal textures, such as "color," "clarity," "airiness," "grittiness," and so on, to tame or enhance your sound and make it more interesting.

- Increase or decrease air pressure to trigger new combinations of overtones within your instrument.

- If relevant, adjust your grip on the microphone and the distance it's kept from your mouth to capture and manipulate the sound of your voice.

OFF STAGE: For this off stage solution, you can try an *exploratory* exercise, rather than a lyric replacement. To do this, deliver the song with radically misplaced emotional intent. If it's a sad song, sing the same melody as happily as you possibly can. If it's a peaceful song, sing it as angrily and intensely as you possibly can. The objective is to dispel any programmed boundaries you may or may not be capable of expressing within the rails of a melody. Here, you can explore multiple shades, styles, or even genres outside of the vocal gym, giving yourself permission to play and be fearlessly creative. After allowing yourself to break the rules, reconnect to the original intent of the song and you may find it much easier to express as you intended.

Articulation Solutions

ON STAGE: As you may recall, the vocal articulators are collectively one of the four fundamental elements that make up our instrument. Regardless of the language you're singing in, if you are unable to make the words comprehensible and independent of pitch, volume, or tone, try these temporary solutions:

- Exaggerate the words, particularly the consonants, which will help tell the story and assist in defining the melody.

- Simplify your *tone* to help reduce any vocal tension and minimize potential overuse of the articulatory muscles.

- Utilize more body language and facial expressions to tell the song's story, which will also help to keep the audience engaged and connected.

- When permitted, decrease the tempo of the song to help facilitate the words and provide more opportunities to enunciate clearly.

OFF STAGE: To focus on the independence between the tongue and jaw muscles, we can do a lyric replacement exercise with "Lä" and "Gä." Try rotating back and forth between these two sounds for each new syllable and note. The difficulty will be relative to how well you're able to keep the jaw in a relaxed open "ä" position. A two fingertips distance between your top and bottom teeth is a good goal to maintain. Also, the tip of the tongue should fall forward to gently touch your bottom lip, with the exception of a normally placed "L." This means the rear of the tongue will have to stretch and lift to form a "G" without disturbing the front. Using a mirror to monitor these unusual postures will greatly speed up the coordination process.

Strength Solutions

ON STAGE: The stamina and stability of your voice will be tested when performing night after night. This is especially true when under extreme circumstances such as being sick, dealing with poor stage conditions, or high-stress levels. If your voice isn't holding up, be conscious of how you use and maintain it before and after each performance. Don't be shy to let friends and family know you wish to communicate via text, especially in loud environments, in order to gain more vocal rest. If relevant, you may also want to consider being strategic with your song choices and the order in which they are performed:

- Lower your volume where and when you can within the melody to reserve *strength* and let the microphone do the work for you.

- Intentionally jump from one vocal register to another, wherever appropriate to do so, to minimize tension and fatigue.

- Modify or simplify your tone of voice in order to mask or avoid vocal instabilities.

- When possible, extend instrumental sections and utilize backup singers, or even your audience, during loud, repetitive, parts of a song to help pace your voice.

OFF STAGE: Similar to what we did with our off stage *Breathing Exercise*, we can target *strength* by replacing each syllable and note change with a loud "Hä." The increase in air pressure and open formant will require a tremendous amount of vocal stability, stamina, and breath management. Remember to apply all of the *Throga Guidelines* to help stay in a perpetual state of awareness. This will help make the exercise more efficient for subconscious programming and be beneficial to your singing, beyond the immediate song.

If you're unable to sing your chosen song well and without excess tension, even after repeated practice and exploring the suggestions above, it's okay to shift your focus to other songs. Particularly if it's for an audition or performance right around the corner. It's not to say that you should never sing the song again; it just may not be suited to highlight you and your instrument at this time. In the interim, you can still practice it for fun and as a challenge in your personal development.

Mistakes On Stage

Once you're feeling confident with your song choices and are rehearsing for the stage, there's one more thing to prepare; how to handle mistakes. When mistakes happen on stage, and they will, your immediate response should be to convince your audience that the error was done intentionally. If you forget a lyric, make up a new one. If you miss a note, bend it into place. If your voice cracks, make it sound passionate. In other words, don't let your listeners know that you made a mistake in the first place. Let your facial expressions, body language, and continued vocal delivery appear as though these were *choices* you wanted to share, not what you needed to do in response to environmental distractions, imbalanced behaviors, or programs in progress.

Your objective is not to be perfect. Your objective is to provoke emotion within your listeners. This is, by definition, what makes singing an art form, rather than just skilled athleticism. If the mistake is too big to brush off, such as falling off the stage or singing a different song than the band behind you, laugh it off! This will give your audience permission to enjoy a special moment of vulnerability *with* you, instead of feeling embarrassed *for* you. From there, steer them back to the original intent of the song as soon as possible. Trying to hide or deny a "pink elephant" on stage will only bring more attention to it.

This relationship between mind and art is fascinating. Take another medium, such as painting. If you were to ask someone if they liked a painting you just made, they may genuinely comment on how beautiful it is, how it makes them feel, point out a color or a brushstroke that grabs their attention, as well as congratulate you on the success of your vision. However, if you were to show the same person, the same painting, and tell them that you're not finished with it yet; they will bombard you with opinions on your color choices, subject matter, perspective, depth of shading, attention to detail, and so on and so forth.

This person isn't being mean-spirited or overly critical. They are only responding to a natural sequence of mental permissions that you set in motion; searching what, where, how, and why something might need to change in order to reach completion. Their dissatisfaction is in response to your own. The reality is, your audience will accept whatever it is you present to them as a final version. If it happens to align with their pre-programming, or "taste," they will embrace and even praise you for it. So whether you sang the song exactly as you originally intended or not, is nearly irrelevant. Make the "mistake" a part of your art and allow yourself, and your audience, to enjoy it.

These mistakes, vocal imbalances and other stage experiences will play a pivotal role in your overall development. Not only will they motivate you to practice more, they will help you discover dimensional imbalances that may have otherwise hid in the shadows of your dominant programming. In the next chapter, *Vocal-Exercise Mapping*, we'll explore how to create and customize exercises to fine-tune your instrument.

Diagnostics and Solutions Summary

- The *Throga Guidelines* don't apply when singing a song.

- When diagnosing your voice, be observant without interfering, so you can identify which dimension(s) needs to be addressed.

- Adapt the song to fit your voice whenever and wherever possible, so that it highlights your unique vocal characteristics.

- To take on specific song challenges, bring the melody of the song into the vocal gym by replacing the lyric with an appropriate formant and feature.

- Your objective when singing is not to be "perfect," it's to provoke an emotional response.

- Make "mistakes" a part of your performance.

- Mistakes are needed to grow as a singer and performer.

Vocal Exercise Mapping

Chapter XII

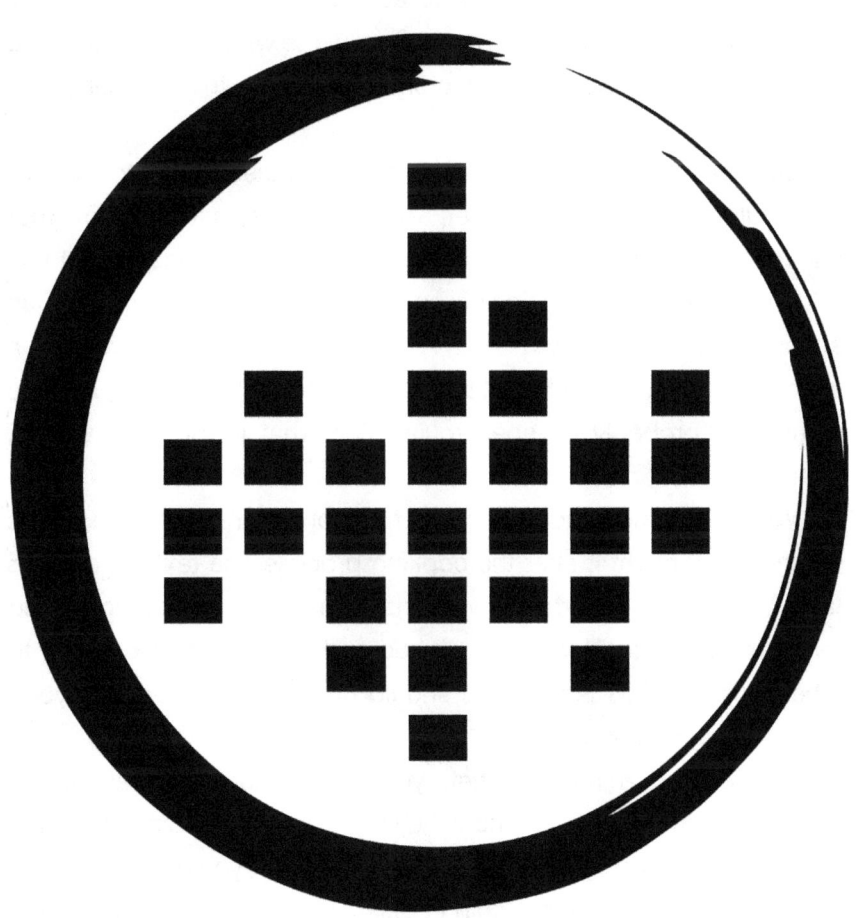

Have you ever thought to yourself, "I wonder how I can create my own vocal exercises."

No?

Well, you're not alone. Few have ventured to map this out. Not because it doesn't hold relevance to vocal development, but because most of our institutions train us to accept what is being presented, rather than to question it. This is especially true when we're young and impressionable, creating a trajectory of behavior that we carry into adulthood.

Let's say, for example, you were taking a master class to improve your culinary skills as a baker. After a quick taste test of your chocolate chip cookie dough batter, the instructor suggests that you add more salt than the recipe called for. Given that the instructor is an accomplished chef, you're likely to follow his instruction without a second thought. After all, he knows what he's talking about, and the results will probably be spectacular. But what if you were to ask, "Why?"

What effect does adding more of this one ingredient have on the others? How might it alter the cooking process, the texture, and the taste? And more importantly, what happens when you go home and try it for yourself; will you know when and how much salt to add to other recipes? This is why you should be asking questions beyond what's being presented.

To become a master chef, you must understand all of the components of a recipe and how they interact in order to get the result you're looking for on a consistent basis. This way, you not only master the art of baking chocolate chip cookies, you'll be able to apply that knowledge and experience to perfecting other recipes as well. Understanding the components of a vocal exercise will provide you with the same type of accuracy in the vocal gym. It will also expand your ability to modify and adapt to the conditions and intentions of the moment to get desired results.

The total nutritional value in any recipe can be measured by its collective totals in fat, protein, carbohydrates, calories, vitamins, fiber, and so forth. The same can be said about the nutritional value of any vocal exercise. It too can be broken down into how it benefits each of the 7 Dimensions. By varying the following six components, or ingredients, we can adjust the impact on any particular dimension using the following formula. A vocal exercise is:

Vocal Exercise =
Formant + *Feature + Pattern + Volume + Tempo + *Variable

*Feature and variable are optional components, depending on how you want the exercise to benefit you. For example, removing the feature of an exercise would be like removing the chocolate chips from your recipe. It's still a cookie, but that one modification will result in very different nutrition totals, changing how it fuels and balances the needs of your body. So much in fact, it would require an entirely different title, perhaps a "sugar cookie."

The nutritional totals of a vocal exercise can be measured by how much they affect each dimension. You've already seen this in action with the 7DS graphs displayed for each chapter exercise, illustrating the totals of how much each dimension will benefit the needs of your voice.

Of course, not everyone wants to be a master chef. Some just love to eat. That's okay too! Here, in our vocal kitchen, we are about to dissect the components of an exercise. This is key for those of you who are teachers or are curious about how exercises can be systematically broken down. This will amplify your ability to make the right adjustments within your practice and in the practice of others.

However, for many singers, this information may be perceived as an "extra." A dessert, if you will. If you're feeling full, go ahead and move on to the next chapter to officially begin a new journey with Throga. You can always return to this chapter when you're hungry for more.

"It is by going down into the abyss that we recover the treasures of life. Where you stumble, there lies your treasure."

- Joseph Campbell (1904 - 1987)

The gridded charts below illustrate how each dimension is targeted within an exercise. These charts, or maps, serve as your guide to determine which components should be utilized to construct or refine an exercise. By combining all six pieces of the map, you will uncover the dimensional totals, represented as "X." If X signifies the location of your treasure to improve, it's important to note that treasure maps only lead you to the general vicinity. You will still need to dig a few holes at varying depths to unearth your reward. In other words, it takes time and patience.

To map an exercise, select one item from each of the following component charts to find "X." For instance, if you were back in the kitchen and wanted a cookie with more protein in it, you would choose ingredients that would correspond with that goal. When you're in the vocal gym and want to focus more on *strength*, you would choose one or more components that correspond with that goal as well.

When selecting, remember that every component will affect every dimension, at least to some degree. The darker the shade of grey is within the chart, the more the corresponding dimension will be affected. However, there is still great value in working through exercises that have a light or medium shade of grey in each of the exercises to develop a solid foundation as a vocalist.

← less   more →

A reminder to those of you with previous vocalizing experience; every exercise you've ever done, with good form, has been beneficial to you in some way. What's being presented here is to help you understand HOW they are beneficial, providing more insight as to what you might change, if at all, to continually progress.

Formant

Formant	F	B	I	R	T	A	S
lip-trill (as in "brrr")	■	▨	░	░	░	■	░
m (as in "hum")	■	░	░	░	░	▨	░
ng (as in "tongue")	■	░	░	░	░	▨	░
z (as in "buzz")	▨	■	▨	▨	░	■	░
ā (as in "day")	▨	▨	░	░	░	░	░
ē (as in "see")	▨	░	░	░	░	░	░
ä (as in "father")	░	■	▨	■	■	▨	■
ō (as in "no")	░	▨	▨	░	░	░	░
oo (as in "boot")	■	░	░	░	░	▨	░
ŭ (as in "gum")	▨	■	▨	▨	▨	░	░
multi-formants		▨	▨	▨	■	■	▨

1st Component: A formant, in the context of a vocal exercise, is a sustainable and identifiable sound created by the shape of the vocal tract, also known as our resonator. Each sound listed in the chart has its own resonant pattern due to the amplification and absorption of frequencies while generating different degrees of backpressure.

Selecting the formants of an exercise is like selecting the flour you want in your cookie recipe. Every type and brand of flour will have an impact on how the cookie tastes, rises, and fuels your body. Make a single selection from the familiar formants above, based on your current condition and dimensional goals.

Feature	F	B	I	R	T	A	S
NONE (optional)							
vocal fry	▓	■		░	■		░
B or **D**	░	░			░	▓	
P or **T**	░	░			░	■	
G or **K**	▓	▓	░		▓	■	
L	░				░	▓	
H		■	▓	░			■
M, **N**, or **NG**	▓				░	░	
S	░	░	░			■	░
Z		▓	░	░	░	▓	
multi-features	▓	▓			■	■	░

2nd Component: A feature is a sound that can be added to, or be an interruption of, a formant. Features alter subglottic pressure and resonant patterns created by the position or temporary movement of the articulatory muscles within the vocal tract, similar to formants.

Think of features as an optional "spice" in our recipe analogy, in which you can add or modify its total nutritional value. Or in this case, dimensional targeting. Feel free to explore other features to accommodate your objectives as well.

Pattern	F	B	I	R	T	A	S
single note							
< 5th glissando							
> 5th glissando							
< 5th scale							
> 5th scale							
< 5th gliss-scale							
> 5th gliss-scale							

3rd Component: A pattern refers to the order and duration of each note within a given exercise. Patterns can be divided into three basic types, which can also be a combination thereof:

1. **Single notes:** consisting of one selected pitch
2. **Glissandos:** consisting of at least two pitches sliding from one note to another
3. **Intervals:** often referred to as scales, consisting of at least two pitches jumping from one note to another

Generally speaking, a single note will target *strength*, a glissando will target *flexibility* and *range*, and scales will primarily influence the dimension of *intonation*. The complexity of a pattern will also play a role in how much each dimension is affected. If the pattern's overall interval span is less than a fifth (the distance between the first two words of "Twinkle Twinkle Little Star"), it won't assist in targeting *flexibility* and *range* as much as an octave interval span (the distance between the first two notes in "Somewhere Over the Rainbow").

Volume

	F	B	I	R	T	A	S
quiet (< speech)	■	■	■		■		
medium (speech)	■	■		■	■	■	■
loud (> speech)		■	■	■	■	■	■
swells (quiet/loud)		■	■	■	■	■	■

4th Component: Volume refers to the general measurement of decibels (dB) in which an exercise is practiced. Below is a breakdown of approximate decibel levels when singing, relative to your natural tendencies to project when speaking.

Quiet: less than the average speaking voice (under 60 dB)
Medium: the average speaking voice (approx. 60 - 75 dB)
Loud: greater than the average speaking voice (above 75 dB)
Swell: crescendos / decrescendos (spanning a 10+ dB range)

Vocalizing at a quiet volume will make it easier for your vocal folds to stretch and become more flexible, thereby targeting f*lexibility*. On the other side of the spectrum, a loud volume will challenge your voice by having to skillfully manage a significant amount of air for the duration of the exercise, targeting the dimension of *breathing*. In addition, the louder volumes will build *strength*, trigger more overtones (*tone*), challenge *articulation*, and target *range* when working through your passaggio.

Keep in mind that not every volume is available for every formant. For instance, a closed formant such as "n" cannot be naturally projected to the same dB level as an "ā."

7 Dimensions of Singing

Tempo	F	B	I	R	T	A	S
slow (< 76 bpm)	░	■		■	■		■
moderate (76-120)	▓	▓	▓	▓	▓	▓	▓
fast (> 120 bpm)	■		■			■	

5th Component: Musical patterns can be divided into beats per minute (bpm) and tempo refers to the speed at which a pattern is played, based on the bpm. Typically, the slower or longer a vocal exercise is, the more coordination for breath management (*breathing*), and vocal stability (*strength*) is required. Conversely, the faster or shorter an exercise is, the easier it is to control airflow, and the more responsive (*flexibility*) the vocal folds have to be. The same can be said for a still or slow-moving yoga stance, versus a quick, flowing movement from one asana to another.

Depending on how a pattern is constructed, the tempo used in an exercise can range anywhere from 40 to 200 bpm. Commonly used terms to categorize tempos are:

Largo: 40 - 60 bpm
Larghetto: 60 - 66 bpm
Adagio: 66 - 76 bpm
Andante: 76 - 108 bpm

Moderato: 108 - 120 bpm
Allegro: 120 - 168 bpm
Presto: 168 - 200 bpm
Prestissimo: 200+ bpm

When improvising an exercise, the relativity of it *feeling* slow, moderate, or fast is usually enough to generate accurate results. That said, it can be extremely helpful to clap along or use a metronome to make sure you don't inadvertently speed up to avoid running out of air or slow down to make pitches or diction easier.

Variable	F	B	I	R	T	A	S
NONE (optional)							
low larynx		■		■	■	■	
tongue forward		■		■	■	■	■
head circles	■			■	■		
lying down	■	■		■			■
stretch	■		■	■	■		
cardio		■	■	■	■		■

6th Component: Vocalizing is generally practiced in a relaxed upright, sitting or standing, position. Intentionally modifying this posture, or adding a physical action while vocalizing, can assist in finalizing your exercise map.

However, it is recommended to initially attempt the exercise without any variables. This allows you to concentrate on the fundamental aspects of the exercise. Once you feel comfortable with the first five components, you can assess whether any of the optional variables should be introduced. When applying a variable, it is important to approach them mindfully and maintain proper form:

Low Larynx: Release the "swallowing muscles" directly above the larynx to allow your larynx to sink into a yawn-like position. This will assist with the development of *tone* and *range*. You should notice not only the timbre of your voice change with additional low overtones, but also the movement of your larynx releasing downward. Though an unusual sound and feeling, at no point should there be a feeling of force or discomfort. Additionally, you can look into a mirror or feel your throat to confirm this action when first exploring it.

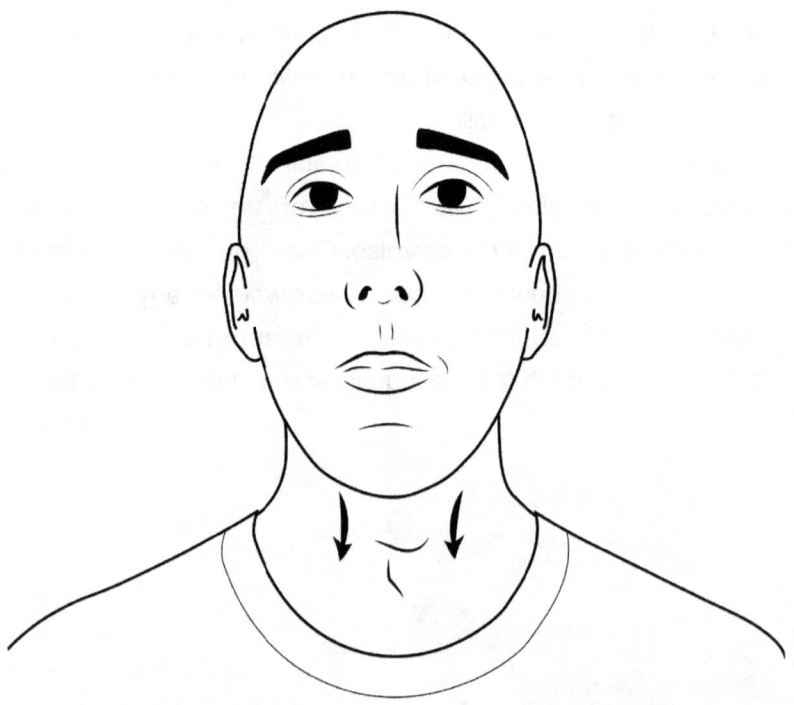

The Throga Technique

Tongue Forward: Bring the tip of your tongue forward to gently touch your bottom lip, draping the bottom teeth. Though awkward in practice, this extension of the tongue will assist in developing muscular independence, ideal for *articulation* and *tone* when singing. By resting a finger just outside your mouth, you can also have your tongue reach further forward to touch it for additional tactile feedback.

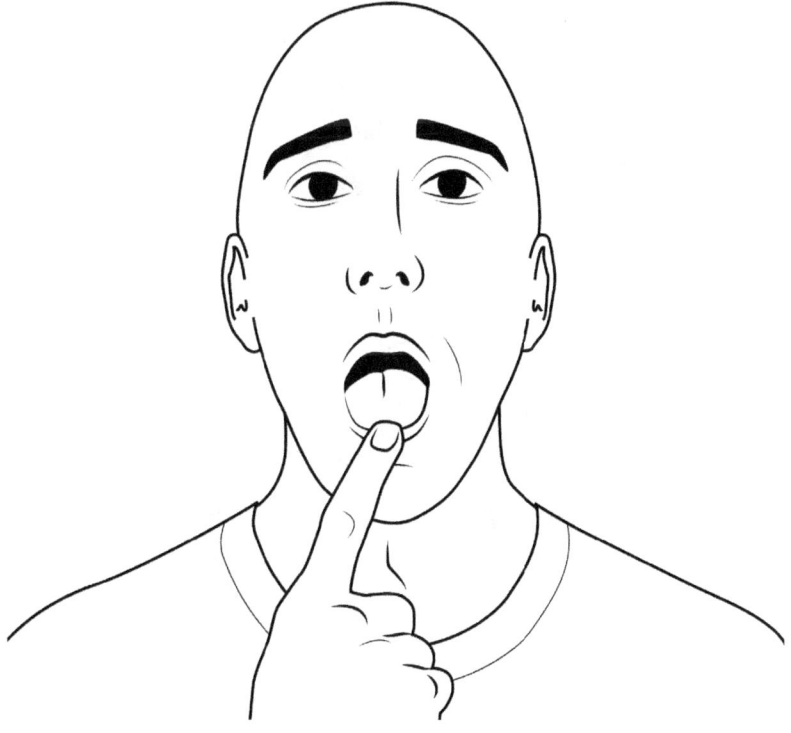

Head Circles: Maintain a small circular motion with your head in a slow and steady manner while vocalizing. Keeping the larger exterior muscles busy with this light neck and shoulder massage will assist in neutralizing interior stress and help to focus on the smaller muscles we want to target for phonation. Using a mirror for visual feedback, consistency, and accuracy is highly recommended.

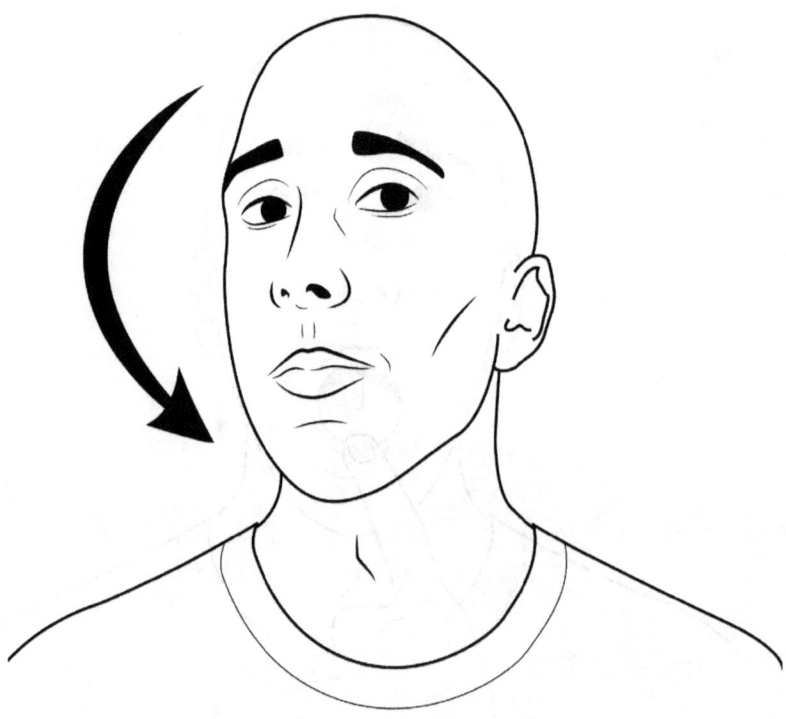

Lie Down: Lie down on a hard surface with your feet flat on the floor and your head supported with a small pillow or rolled up towel. This gravitational shift will cause your body to redistribute its weight, reduce muscular tensions, and amplify your awareness for *breathing*. Once you're able to gain vocal balance in this position, try reproducing it with the same degree of minimal effort when upright.

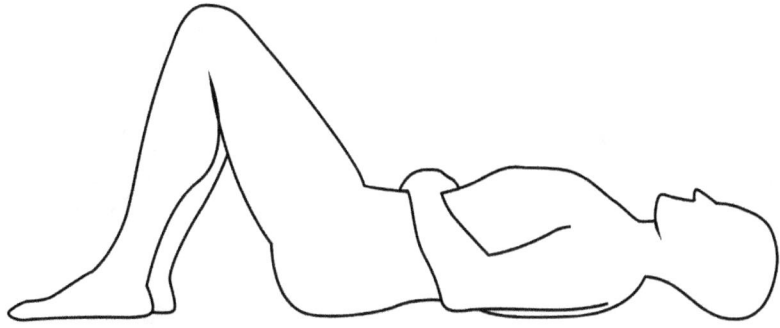

Stretch: Practice yoga, tai chi, or any basic body stretches while vocalizing. This will provide a healthy physical distraction from stress and overthinking, often freeing the body with a positive impact on *flexibility*, *range*, and *tone*. Reactionary movements such as bouncing a ball off the walls, floor, and ceiling will also encourage you to stay loose and responsive.

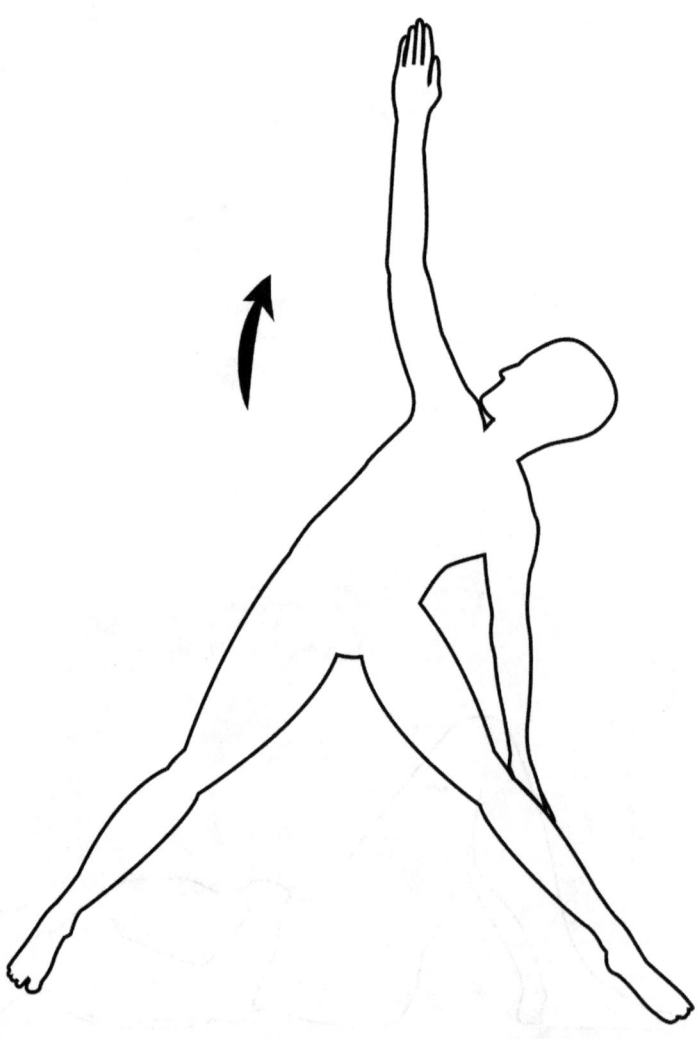

Cardio: Doing a light jog, stair climbing, jumping jacks, cycling, or dancing in time with an exercise will challenge *breathing* and overall stability of the voice (*strength*). Aerobic activity demands a high percentage of oxygen-rich blood to the muscles and forces your body to manage everything more efficiently while attempting to sing. This is especially helpful to singers who are highly active or dance on stage.

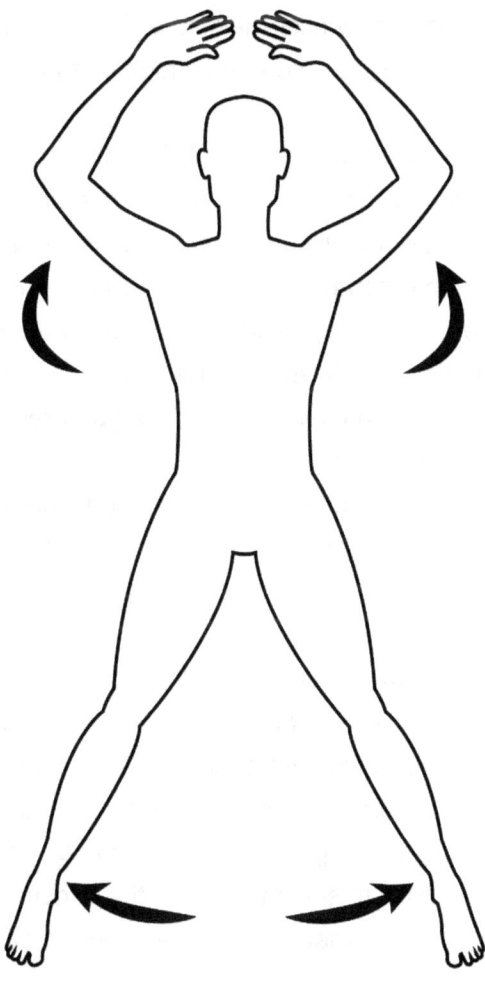

Having read all of the component options, let's put them to the test with an exercise of your choice. Any exercise is fine. It can be one you tried in an earlier chapter, or maybe something you learned in the choir or heard online. When you think of one, go back to the first component chart and find the formant in your chosen exercise. Next, identify the feature within the exercise, if there is one. After that, select the relative pattern.

At this point, you should start to notice how the dimensions collaborate from just these first few components. Continue through the remaining charts while making a mental note as to which dimensions are being targeted and which ones may not be targeted at all.

Are you surprised by the results? Is the exercise you use for warmups better suited for the dimension of *articulation*? Is your *intonation* exercise actually a *strength* exercise in disguise? You may discover that some components confirm what you already believe to be true, while others may strike you as strange or conflicting with previous experiences. Given that a single component can radically modify the focus of an exercise, perhaps you are only one selection away from your intention.

Let's explore this idea further. Take one component from the exercise you just analyzed. Tempo, for example. Now try vocalizing the same exercise at a dramatically different speed than you did originally to see how it feels.

Did that recalibrate your focus within the exercise? Did it shift the challenge from one dimension to another? If you believe an exercise to be contradictory to what your map suggests, there are a couple of things to consider. First, is that the exercise may still be beneficial to your subconscious programming, having a positive effect on improving your ability to sing overall and the dimensions you intended to address. Second, is that you may have underestimated the power of the placebo effect, which is a simulated treatment that takes advantage of the body's self-healing and self-correcting abilities.

The reality is, just believing that an exercise will help you sing better, has a decent chance in being successful. Sugar pills have been known to cure pain, disease, and even thwart off cancer cells. The mind is powerful. The problem with placebos though, is that it only works about one third of the time. This is why any exercise, even done poorly, can often have a short-term positive effect. However, when you attach physiological facts and reason to your belief in an exercise's ability to help you, the percentage of success is significantly increased, affording more and more opportunities to improve within your practice.

Let's review.

You know the difference between being on stage and in the vocal gym. You know what the seven dimensions of singing are and which ones to focus on in your training. And now you've learned how to create and fine-tune an exercise to target those dimensions.

In the final chapter, we will answer two of the most commonly asked questions in regard to any type of training: "How often do I need to practice?" and "How do I know if I'm improving?"

Vocal-Exercise Mapping Summary

- Vocal-Exercise Mapping is a segmented layout of components and their relative values for each dimension.

- Understanding the components that make up an exercise will allow you to create or modify them as needed.

- All vocal exercises consist of up to six components: formant, feature, pattern, volume, tempo, and variable, where feature and variable are optional.

- Vocal exercises can be measured by the degree in which they affect or target the seven dimensions.

- Changing a single component can alter how an exercise will affect your training.

- Any exercise, done with good form, will benefit your vocal development in some way.

- Understanding how an exercise will help you is more fruitful than just believing that it will.

It's the Journal, Not the Destination
Chapter XIII

7 Dimensions of Singing

Every journey has a beginning, filled with hope and desire to reach a new destination. But not every journey has to end. Your quest to sing as you imagine yourself singing may have begun long ago, but your adventure continues every time you take in a new concept, write or refine a subconscious program, or expand your belief in your capacity to excel. Reading this book, for instance, brought you a new set of tools. It's taken you further along in your vocal journey, teleporting you to new places in your mind and teaching you to see yourself through new lenses.

So how do we know in which direction to continue?

"We mark the trees during the day and follow the stars at night."

This poetic and somewhat cryptic thought derives from a parallel between your journey and the heroes woven into every great myth, folklore, fairytale, and bedtime story around the world; the story of an unassuming individual going on an unexpected adventure that one day becomes a hero by overcoming perilous odds to help, save, or inspire others.

In the story of *Hansel and Gretel*, two young children left a trail of breadcrumbs deep into the forest, so they could find their way home again. As a vocalist, trying to remember every exercise you've done at every turn can be disorientating. Your subconscious will follow behind you and consume your short-term memory breadcrumbs, getting you lost in a forest of pre-programmed behaviors. Instead, you'll want to mark the trees to avoid going in circles and losing your way. In times of frustration, you can look to the stars, using the Throga tools, to re-orientate yourself.

Use the pages of your new vocal journal as your trees. You can tell your story by keeping track of where you've been, where you are in your practice, as well as your progress. This will help you to stay motivated and to avoid tempting shortcuts that would cost you in the long run. We all know the cost of eating from the witches' sponge cake cottage! However, unlike our fabled friends, Hansel and Gretel, you don't want to return to where you started. You'll want to continue the adventure, creating new maps, finding more treasures, and celebrating new beginnings.

In the following sections, we'll discuss how to keep a vocal journal, how often you should practice to reach your goals, and how to examine whether or not you're improving.

Vocal Gym Journal

The *Vocal Gym Journal* consists of two templates (available for download in the 🔊 **7DS Book Media**). The first template, labeled "Vocal Gym Exercises," is a master list of your vocal exercises, which identifies each of the exercise's components. The second template, labeled "Vocal Gym Journal," is for keeping track of your daily training and progress.

In the following example, each of the chapter exercises from this book has been broken down into their respective components. Over the next two weeks, you can target a variety of dimensions by adding one new exercise of your own each day, using the "practice tracks" on Throga's website. This way, in just two weeks' time, you'll have a total of twenty-one exercises on your master list to keep your training exciting and productive, by continuously rotating and modifying exercises daily.

Vocal Gym Exercises

#	Formant	Feature	Pattern	Volume (M L S)	Tempo (S M F)	Variable	7DS (B I R T A S)
1	ɛ	M/vocal fry	glissando - full range	✓ M L S	S M ✓	tongue	✓ B I R T A S
2	ɛ	H	single note - triplets	✓ M L S	S M ✓	-	F ✓ R T A S
3	z	-	pulse - 13243534231	✓ M L S	S ✓ F	-	F B ✓ R T A S
4	ä	-	glissando - octave	Q M ✓ S	✓ M F	-	F D I ✓ T A S
5	ü	G	scale - 1358531	Q ✓ L S	S ✓ F	low larynx	F B I R ✓ A S
6	ä ɛ ä ö öö	multi	scale - 123454321	Q M L ✓	S M ✓	-	F B I R T ✓ S
7	multi	-	single note - counting	Q M L S	S M F	-	F B I R T A ✓
8				Q M L S	S M F		F B I R T A S
9				M L S	S M F		R T A S

In the next example, the start of a Vocal Gym Journal has already been filled out. Here, it references exercises, potential modifications, the targeted dimensions, and how much time was spent doing them.

The Throga Technique

Utilizing the first three chapter exercises for *flexibility*, *breathing*, and *intonation* is a great way to begin journaling. You can then explore the remaining chapter exercises and introduce others you've been taught, or created, on the following days. Regardless of the dimensions you choose to work on, always starting your training with a *flexibility* exercise or two is extremely beneficial.

Vocal Gym Journal

Date	Exercise	Modifications	7DS	Time
Jan 1	1	no vocal fry	✓ B I R T A S	7 mins
	2	-	F ✓ I R T A S	7 mins
	3	-	F B ✓ R T A S	14 mins
Jan 2	1	did yoga while vocalizing	✓ B I R T A S	7 mins
	4	quiet volume and added "head circle"	✓ B I ✓ T A S	14 mins
	4	-	F B I ✓ T A S	3 mins
	2	mid volume	F ✓ I R T A S	7 mins
Jan 3	6	quiet volume with "M" feature only	✓ B I R T ✓ S	14 mins
	3	-	F B ✓ R T A S	21 mins
	7	used "Ha" instead of numbers	F ✓ I R T A ✓	3 mins
	7	-	F B I R T A ✓	7 mins
Jan 4	4	quiet and faster than normal	✓ B I R T A S	7 mins
	3	no pulse (legato)	✓ B ✓ R T A S	10 mins
	6	loud volume and all "ā" formant	F B I R ✓ ✓ S	14 mins
	5	-	F B I R ✓ A S	7 mins
			B I R T A S	7 mins

Marking the dimensions will make it easy to see which ones you've addressed in your practice. As you may have noticed in the journal example, the dimension of *tone* was neglected for several days before it was targeted. The more time you spend journaling, the more precise your practice will become and the better organized your subconscious programming will be.

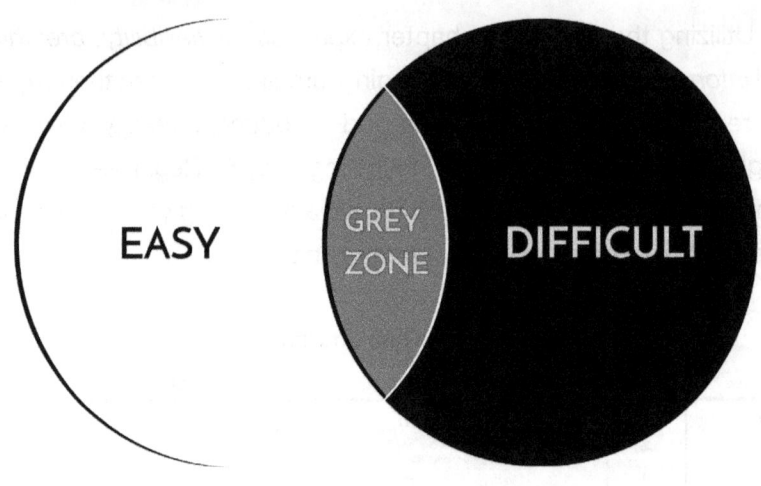

To optimize your training, you'll want to practice in the "Grey Zone," between "easy" and "difficult," as shown in the Venn diagram above. The goal is to spend as much time as possible in the overlapping space, where these two concepts intersect. Though exercises that are easy or difficult will have benefits and should be occasionally explored, they generally hinder progress. The reason for this is that if training is too easy, our subconscious tends to run the show and we become complacent in our practice. If training is too difficult, we respond with unnecessary frustration and tension, which reinforces negative behaviors in our singing. Mindful vocalizing, the "middle way," is ideal.

"Give a man a fish and you feed him for a day.
Teach a man to fish and you feed him for a lifetime."

- Unknown

Since your voice is with you 24 hours a day and a teacher isn't, no one is there to tell you when to switch to a louder volume, change to a slower tempo, or graduate to a new pattern every time you practice. This is why understanding how to access and sustain your time in the grey zone, with or without a teacher, is essential to your journey. It's also where the benefit of journaling comes into play. It will alarm you or alert you of what you need to work on and if any adjustments are needed. Even a single modification will help keep your mind focused and your voice responsive.

Aside from *flexibility* during warmups, there's no need to dedicate a lot of attention towards a dimension you might already excel at, as each dimension will always be partially addressed. However, if you're truly struggling and frustrated with an exercise, it indicates that at least one of the dimensions being targeted may be overly challenged. When this happens, try altering one of the components at a time to determine the best approach to stay out of the difficult and into the grey.

If you feel the exercises in this book are too difficult, don't get discouraged. Every singer has room to improve in every dimension. No exceptions. Take on one at a time, in the order that they're presented and follow the suggestions in the respective chapter to simplify the exercise as you build your foundation. If *none* of the book exercises feel challenging, double-check that you're following every one of the *Throga Guidelines* before exploring optional components. Remember, you're on a treasure hunt, actively seeking opportunities to improve. Over time, you will have the wisdom to make quick and precise modifications in your practice, which will allow you to continuously progress.

How Often Should I Practice?

If you're unable to satisfy your artistic endeavors by trial and error alone, quality vocal training will be necessary. How much time you spend practicing is only as effective as how mindful your practice actually is. For training the mind and body, one hour a day of focused vocalizing will create new positive behaviors in a relatively short period of time. This does NOT include the countless hours you'll be spending singing, songwriting, performing, or tracking in the studio if you're pursuing a full-time career.

If one hour a day seems like too much, keep in mind that this is no different from prioritizing any other passion you may want to turn into a profession. How many hours does a dancer commit to their craft to earn the title of "professional?" How many years does it take to become a noted painter, poet, or songwriter? Like anything else in life, the more you put into it, the more you will get out of it.

"If I miss one day's practice, I notice it. If I miss two days' practice, the critics notice it. If I miss three days' practice, the public notices it."

- Franz Liszt (1811 - 1866)

As we discussed earlier, you can access the vocal gym at the speed of thought. Which, unfortunately, means you can exit just as quickly. The moment you start thinking about having to reply to a text message, do the laundry, finish the yard work, or order something online, you are no longer present. This is why it's often ideal to work in concentrated sessions of about 20 minutes at a time.

Every 20 minutes, simply shift your attention to a new dimension or introduce a new variable with your current exercise. You can also take breaks in between these sessions, spanning anywhere from a few minutes to several hours. Just as long as you keep in touch with *flexibility*-based activities to remain loose. This can include casually vocalizing song melodies, scales, or glissandos at low volumes throughout your range.

All of the "practice tracks" in the book media are roughly 7 minutes in length, which accommodates this approach by doing three exercises per session, or nine for a full hour. You can also repeat the same tracks, while making small modifications to the components as needed, to keep the training fresh.

On performance days, whether you'll be on stage or in the studio, it's recommended you modify your warmups accordingly. As a general rule, the length of your training should be inversely proportionate to the number of songs you'll be singing. So if you have a grueling four-hour gig ahead of you, or an all-day speaking event, try a short warmup focusing on *flexibility*. If, however, you have a one-song audition or short performance at a wedding, address all seven dimensions with a long warmup to make sure your voice is at its peak when the moment comes.

How Do I Know If I'm Improving?

Nature provides the best examples of growth and transformation. Have you ever stopped to admire a caterpillar slowly dragging itself across a leaf? It's a strange looking creature with some intricate patterns on its back, barely hinting at its wondrous and colorful potential. At some point in its life, a metamorphosis takes place and the caterpillar wraps itself into a cocoon. To us spectators, as we go by, this small brown shell hanging from a leaf may seem rather uninteresting or ordinary. But every day, the shell slowly changes in shape, size, and color, as the creature beneath the surface works tirelessly towards its goal.

As for you, the shape, size, and color of your voice can be measured by the increasing average of successful intentional moments. A combination of senses can be used to witness this: You might feel less strain in your throat when singing high notes, hear yourself match the pitches of a melody more consistently, or have a stronger sense of self-confidence in your practice. However, if you don't feel you are progressing, make sure you're not skipping basic qualifiers for development by asking yourself these questions:

Health: Are you continuously hydrated, getting enough sleep, and avoiding trauma to the folds such as coughing or yelling?

Tools: Are you using your map (7DS) and compass (*Throga Guidelines*) to target the correct dimensions with good form?

Practice: Are you practicing mindfully every day? Or just every so often when it's casually convenient?

Sometimes, it can be difficult to distinguish what you've improved upon when being so close to your voice. An easy way to monitor progress is to use the Vocal Profile on Throga's website. Then you can go back and visually see how you've been progressing over time.

The Throga Technique

Another way is to occasionally record yourself singing a select song, and then go back to listen every few weeks or months to compare and examine which dimension(s) you may need work on. Using a simple voice-recording app will do fine. Just be sure to label the dates.

"When you come to see you are not as wise today as you thought you were yesterday, you are wiser today."

- Anthony DeMello (1931 – 1987)

At times, you may feel you're leveling off in your progress or even taking a step backward. If this happens, even though you're applying all of the tools presented in this book and practicing daily, fear not. As your skills advance, so will your awareness. Awareness is impartial. It doesn't shed light on the things you wish to see and cast a shadow over the things you don't. It burns equally bright on all seven dimensions, illuminating the imperfections and imbalances we seek to improve.

Every day, you wake up with a new version of yourself. This is due to the experience and knowledge you gain from the day before, general health, and environmental conditions. Therefore, slight modifications will be needed to sing with consistent results, let alone get better. In *Vocal Exercise Mapping*, we compared the vocal gym to a kitchen. Imagine waking up in a new kitchen every day, having to cook the exact same batch of cookies. You might find this more challenging than expected. Are you using the same brand of ingredients as the day before? What is the humidity and the temperature of the cupboards where they're kept? Did the thickness of your cooking tray change? Did you have to use cooking spray today instead of your normal wax paper?

The multiples of variations from the quality and measurement of each ingredient to the process of cooking, are infinite. The same is with your vocal practice. The more skillful you are at navigating the *7 Dimensions of Singing*, the more skilled and reliable your voice will become. However, if journaling doesn't seem practical for you, try to at least remember and apply these two things: (1) rotate and change up your exercises every day and (2) PRACTICE, PRACTICE, PRACTICE... and then practice some more.

Whether you're committed to vocalizing once a month or several times a day, never forget the reason you started training your voice in the first place; your love of singing. This is the ultimate motivational tool to keep forging ahead along your journey.

Returning to the example of the caterpillar in its cocoon, the caterpillar carries the same DNA as it does when it reemerges as a butterfly. But it can only become a butterfly if it makes the necessary preparations and develops the coordination and strength needed to break free from its shell. You too have the capacity to transform. You can either spend your time looking up at the sky with envy, or you can nourish your aspirations to take flight.

Regardless of wherever your vocal goals may lie, or where your journey may take you, learning to balance your voice will enrich your life and add healthy new aspects to the inner self. So remember:

Practice.

Sing.

And fly.

It's the Journal, Not the Destination Summary

- Your journey in vocal development will last for as long as you take in new information to challenge and refine your skills.

- The purpose of keeping a vocal journal is to not lose sight of where you are and in which direction you need to go.

- Do exercises that keep you in the "grey zone," which is halfway between too easy and too difficult.

- Keep a master list of your exercises, so you can easily rotate them to keep your training fresh and effective.

- Begin training with *flexibility* before moving to the dimensions you find most challenging.

- Always apply the *Throga Guidelines* and change only one component at a time to make adjustments.

- Serious singers should vocalize at least an hour every day.

- Divide your practice time into 20-minute segments to keep a steady focus.

- Don't be discouraged if you don't notice immediate changes.

- Record yourself singing a song and archive it, so you can compare it weeks or months later to hear your progress.

- The more quality time you spend training your voice, the more obvious your growth will be when you sing.

Glossary of Terms

Vocal coaches, speech pathologists, otolaryngologists and other specialists use a variety of terms, both medically and metaphorically, to aid in their communication with a vocalist. The following descriptions are intended to provide straightforward and literal translations of key words and terminologies within the context of this book and their relationship to the vocal instrument.

Abdominal Muscles *(ab-dä-mə-nəl mə-səls)***:** a group of muscles used to stabilize the body and work in conjunction with the diaphragm and intercostal muscles for the dimension of *breathing*, which include the external obliques, internal obliques, transversus abdominis, and rectus abdominis located in the abdomen

Abduction *(ab-dək-shən)***:** the action of separating the vocal folds

Actuator *(ak-chə-wā-tər)*: air pressure from the lungs (outgoing breath) that triggers the vibration of the vocal folds

Adduction *(ə-dək-shən)***:** the action of bringing the vocal folds together

Adrenaline *(ə-dre-nə-lən)***:** a hormone released by the adrenal glands as part of the "fight or flight" mechanism, allowing for a temporary increase in strength and speed of reflexes

Alveoli *(al-vē-ə-lī)*: the millions of tiny sacs located in the lungs, which oxygen molecules pass through before entering the bloodstream and from which carbon dioxide is released

Amygdala *(ə-mig-də-lə)*: a structure as part of the limbic system, which regulates a variety of emotions along with our "fight or flight" response

Approximation *(ə-präk-sə-mā-shən)*: the act of bringing the vocal folds close together, from abduction (folds apart) to adduction (folds together) for phonating

Articulator *(är-ti-kyə-lə-tȯr)*: the muscles affiliated with the tongue, jaw, and lips, which refine, disrupt, and shape the sound generated by the vocal instrument's vibrator and resonator

Articulatory Muscles *(är-ti-kyə-lə-tȯr-ē mə-səls)*: the tongue, jaw, and lip muscle groups as part of the vocal tract, which assist in the dimension of *articulation*; **tongue muscles** include the tongue itself (superior, inferior, and transverse longitudinal) and the attached muscles (palatoglossus, styloglossus, hyoglossus, genioglossus, and geniohyoid); **jaw muscles** include the mastacian and mandibular depressors (temporalis, masseters, stylohyoid, pterygoids, digastrics, mylohyoids, and platysmas); **lip muscles** include the orbicularis oris and the surrounding expression muscles (levator labiis, zygomaticus, risorius, buccinator, depressors, and mentalis)

Arytenoid Muscles *(a-rə-tē-nȯid mə-səl)*: muscles of the larynx that swing and pivot for approximation (posterior cricoarytenoid, lateral cricoarytenoid, oblique, and transverse arytenoid), as well as adjustments related to the thickness of the vocal folds

Backpressure *(bak-presh-ər)*: a resistant pressure exerted by air against the narrowing of the vocal tract, making it easier for the thyroarytenoid to disengage and the vocal folds to vibrate

Bernoulli Effect *(bər-nü-lē i-fekt)*: for phonation, this principal of physics brings the outer layers of the vocal folds together in a rapid vibratory pattern when air passes between them at a constant rate

Brain *(brān)*: an organ made of soft tissue located in the skull, which monitors, coordinates, and regulates the actions of the body via the nervous system, including all processes related to singing

Carbon Dioxide *(kär-bən dī-äk-sīd)*: the by-product of the body's usage of oxygen, passed through the alveolus walls,, and released as part of the outgoing breath

Cerebellum *(ser-ə-be-ləm)*: a brain structure responsible for initiating the auditory process and for coordinating and managing voluntary muscular activity such as posture, balance, coordination, speech, and singing

Chest Register *(chest re-jə-stər)*: when the vocal folds are approximated during phonation and in a thicker position than head register

Conscious Mind *(känt-shəs mīnd)*: a part of the nervous system active in the prefrontal cortex, located in the frontal lobe of the brain, which is the center for reasoning, planning, and self-awareness

Cricothyroid *(krīkȯ-thī-rȯid)*: muscle that interacts with the thyroarytenoid (vocalis) muscle, primarily used to adjust tension of the vocal folds for the dimensions of *flexibility*, *intonation*, and *range*, by tilting the thyroid cartilage forward

Diaphragm *(dī-ə-fram)*: dome shaped muscle that divides the abdomen from the thorax (chest), primarily used for inhalation and as an antagonistic relationship with the exhalation muscles during phonation

Dopamine *(dō-pə-mēn)*: a hormone affiliated with the feeling of joy, which the body can release in response to singing

Edema *(i-dē-mə)*: swelling of the vocal folds, often due to friction or infection

Epiglottis *(ep-ə-glät-əs)*: a leaf-shaped cartilage covered in a mucous membrane that closes over the larynx to protect it from foreign particles (food and liquid) when swallowing, which acts as part of the vocal tract, just above the vestibule folds

Epithelium *(e-pə-thē-lē-əm)*: thin outermost layer of the vocal folds, which helps protect them from abrasion caused by the rapid movement of air when breathing and phonating

Exhalation Muscles *(eks-hə-lā-shən mə-səls)*: group of muscles (internal intercostal and abdominal) that work in an antagonistic relationship with the inhalation muscles, used to regulate the release or compression of the lungs to push air outwards

External Intercostal *(ek-stər-nəl in-tər-käs-təl)*: muscles situated between the ribs that expand the lungs to assist with inhalation

External Obliques *(ek-stər-nəl ō-blēks)*: outer part of the abdominal wall that can assist in the control of exhalation

Falsetto Register *(fȯl-se-tō re-jə-stər)*: when the vocal folds are in a thinner position than head register and slightly separated so that mainly just the edges of the vocal folds vibrate

Feature Component *(fē-chər kəm-pō-nənt)*: a vocal exercise component that defines a sound that is added to, or an interruption of, a formant

Formant Component *(fȯr-mənt kəm-pō-nənt)*: a vocal exercise component that defines a sustainable and identifiable sound created by the shape of the vocal tract

Frequency *(frē-kwənt-sē)*: the vibrations of sound-per-second caused by the mucosal wave of the vocal folds

Glottal Shock *(glä-təl shäk)*: a quick collision of the vocal folds, creating a short, non-musical, sound; also known as "glottal stop"

Glottis *(glä-təs)*: the opening between the vocal folds

Hard Palate *(härd pa-lət)*: roof of the oral cavity (mouth) as part of the vocal tract

Head Register *(härd re-jə-stər)*: when the vocal folds are approximated during phonation and in a thinner position than chest register

Hippocampus *(hi-pə-kam-pəs)*: a brain structure as part of the limbic system, associated with converting short-term memory into long-term memory

Hyaluronic Acid *(hīl-yủ-rä-nik a-səd)*: the water-based fluid stored in the LP of the folds, allowing them to vibrate with minimal friction

Hyoid Bone *(hī-òid bōn)*: a "floating" U-shaped bone positioned at the base of the tongue and at the top of the larynx

Hyper-nasal *(hī-pər-nā-zəl)*: the result of too much air passing through the nasal cavities, causing a "thin" or "whiney" sound

Hypo-nasal *(hī-pō-nā-zəl)*: the result of not enough air entering the nasal cavities, causing a "darker," "stuffy-nose," type of sound

Hypothalamus *(hī-pə-tha-lə-məs)*: a brain structure as part of the limbic system, which regulates hormone production, thirst, breathing, mood, pain, pleasure response, and circadian rhythm

Inhalation Muscles *(in-hə-lā-shən mə-səls)*: group of muscles (external intercostal and diaphragm) that work in an antagonistic relationship with the exhalation muscles, used to create a vacuum within the lungs and draw air inward

Internal Intercostal *(in-tər-nəl in-tər-käs-təl)*: muscles situated between the ribs that compress the lungs to assist with exhalation

Internal Obliques *(in-tər-nəl ō-blēks)*: part of the abdominal wall that can assist in the control of exhalation

Lamina Propria *(sü-pər-fi-shəl la-mə-nə prō-pē-ü)*: layers of the vocal folds that vibrate and produce sound, located between the epithelium (outermost layer) and the vocalis muscle (innermost layer), which is primarily made up of highly lubricated elastic fibers; also known as "LP"

Laryngopharynx *(lə-rin-gō-far-iŋks)*: the lowest section of the pharynx (above the larynx), as part of the vocal tract, used to cultivate the dimension of *tone*

Larynx *(ler-iŋks)*: organ located at the top of the trachea with walls of cartilage and muscle, which house the vocal folds for phonation; also responsible for assisting in the action of swallowing, respiration, and can act as a pressure relief valve

Lateral Cricoarytenoid *(la-tə-rəl krī-kȯ-a-rə-tē-nȯid)*: muscles located inside the larynx, partially responsible for bringing the vocal folds together (adduction)

Limbic System *(lim-bik sis-təm)*: a collection of structures in the brain, which manages our pre-rational (unconscious) programming, consisting of emotional, regulatory, and protective operations

Lungs *(ləŋs)*: two large sponge like organs filled with millions of alveoli as part of the vocal instrument's respiratory system and source of air used in the exhalation process for phonating

Mucosal Wave *(myü-kō-zəl wāv)*: a type of vibration created by the wave like action of the vocal folds' outer layers (LP), which pushes air molecules around at various speeds, creating frequencies that the human ear and brain interprets as sound

Nasal Cavities *(nā-zəl ka-və-tēs)*: pathways made of cartilage, between the nasopharynx and nostrils, as part of the vocal instrument's resonator

Nasopharynx *(nā-zō-far-iŋks)*: the highest section of the pharynx (which opens up to the nasal cavities), as part of the vocal tract, used to cultivate the dimension of *tone*

Oblique Arytenoid *(ō-blēk a-rə-tē-nȯid)*: muscles located inside the larynx, partially responsible for bringing the vocal folds together (adduction)

Oral Cavity *(ȯr-əl ka-və-tē)*: open space created by the tongue, oropharynx, soft palate, cheeks, and hard palate as part of the vocal tract; associated more with the dimension of *articulation* than *tone*

Oropharynx *(ȯr-ə-far-iŋks)*: the middle section of the pharynx, as part of the vocal tract, used to cultivate the dimension of *tone*

Overtone *(ō-vər-tōn)*: additional or partial frequencies created from the fundamental sound wave reflecting in the vocal tract (resonator)

Oxygen *(äk-si-jən)*: a colorless, odorless, type of gas mixed into the air we breathe, which the vocal instrument (body) needs to sustain itself

Oxytocin *(äk-sē-tō-sən)*: a hormone affiliated with the feeling of intimacy and attachment, which the body can release in response to singing

Passaggio *(pu-säj-ē-ō)*: the process of transitioning from one vocal register to another; also known as "bridge," "middle," and "mix"

Pattern Component *(pa-tərn kəm-pō-nənt)*: a vocal exercise component that defines the order and duration of each note within a given exercise

Pharynx *(far-iŋks)*: the portion of the throat most affiliated with the dimension of *tone*, which extends from the larynx to the nasal cavity and can be divided into three regions; laryngopharynx, oropharynx, and nasopharynx

Phonate *(fō-nāt)*: any type of vocal sound (singing, speaking, crying, laughing, grunting etc.) created by the vibration of the vocal folds

Pitch *(pich)*: a selected frequency created by a consistent speed of vocal fold vibration

Posterior Cricoarytenoid *(pō-stir-ē-ər krīkȯ-a-rə-tē-nȯid)*: muscles located inside the larynx, primarily responsible for separating the vocal folds (abduction)

Prefrontal Cortex *(prē-frən-təl kȯr-teks)*: located in the frontal lobe of the brain, responsible for self-awareness, reasoning, and planning

Rectus Abdominis *(rek-təs ab-də-mən-is)*: part of the abdominal wall that can assist in the control of exhalation

Resonator *(re-zə-nā-tər)*: the chamber of space in the vocal instrument (vocal tract) that contributes additional resonant frequencies in response to the vocal fold's vibration

Subconscious Mind *(səb-känt-shəs mīnd)*: database of learned information and behaviors in various parts of the brain, which allow the mind to "automatically" process and moderate body actions

Subglottic Pressure *(səb-glät-ik pre-shər)*: air pressure underneath the vocal folds, managed by the exhalation muscles, and the approximation of the folds

Soft Palate *(sòft pa-lət)*: muscle tissue in the upper rear section of the oral cavity, used to channel desired amounts of air (and sound) into the mouth and nose as part of the vocal tract

Tempo Component *(tem-pō kəm-pō-nənt)*: a vocal exercise component that defines the speed at which a pattern is played, measured by beats per minute (bpm)

Thoracic *(thə-ra-sik)*: the space above the diaphragm and enclosed by the ribs (chest), which houses the lungs and heart

Thyroarytenoid *(thī-rō-a-rə-tē-nòid)*: intrinsic muscle of the larynx that can increase and decrease the tension and mass of the vocal folds in an antagonistic relationship with the cricothyroid muscle, directly affiliated with the dimensions of *flexibility*, *intonation*, *range*, and *strength*

Thyroid Cartilage *(thī-ròid kär-tə-lij)*: outer shell of the larynx, often referred to as the "Adam's Apple"

Tone *(tōn)*: resonant patterns (formation of amplified frequencies) created primarily by the shape of the spaces above the larynx (vocal tract); sometimes referred to as "timbre"

Trachea *(trā-kē-ə)*: a windpipe connecting the lungs to the larynx

Transverse Arytenoid *(trans-vərs a-rə-tē-nȯid)*: muscle located inside the larynx, partially responsible for bringing the vocal folds together (adduction)

Transversus Abdominis *(trans-vərs-əs ab-də-mən-is)*: part of the abdominal wall that can assist in the control of exhalation

Unconscious Mind *(ən-kän-shəs mīnd)*: emotional, regulatory, and protective operations in the brain, which takes place unaware to the conscious and subconscious minds

Variable Component *(ver-ē-ə-bəl kəm-pō-nənt)*: a vocal exercise component that defines an intentional modification or action with the body's posture

Vestibule Folds *(ves-tə-byül fōlds)*: a pair of thick folds above the vocal folds in the larynx, designed to manage air pressure, not vibration; also known as "false folds"

Vibrator *(vī-brā-tər)*: the part of the vocal instrument that vibrates (vocal folds) in reaction to the released air pressure from the lungs

Vocal Folds *(vō-kəl fōlds)*: the bottom set of folds in the larynx used for phonation, made of five layers; epithelium, lamina propria (superficial, intermediate, and deep), and the vocalis muscle; also known as "true folds" or "vocal cords"

Vocal Fry Register *(vō-kəl frī re-jə-stər)*: considered to be the lowest vocal register, with an irregular vibration of the folds caused by a lack of subglottic pressure and slight release in the vocal fold's tension

Vocal Register *(vō-kəl re-jə-stər)*: a position of the vocal folds and its interaction with airflow and resonator, which can be categorized as "vocal fry," "chest," "head," "falsetto," and "whistle"

Vocal Tract *(vō-kəl trakt)*: the collective spaces between the vocal folds and the lips and nostrils (pharynx, oral cavity, and nasal cavities), which act as the instrument's resonator

Vocalis *(vō-kā-ləs)*: the medial part of the thyroarytenoid muscle and innermost part of the vocal folds, which cause them to thicken when contracted, playing a significant role in phonation and vocal register positioning

Vocalize *(vō-kə-līz)*: the act of phonating with intent to train and improve skill or coordination of the voice for singing and speaking

Volume Component *(väl-yəm kəm-pō-nənt)*: a vocal exercise component that defines the general measurement of decibels (dB) in which it is practiced

Whistle Register *(hwi-səl re-jə-stər)*: considered to be the highest vocal register, which takes place when the vocal folds are pulled tight with a tiny space for air to travel through, forcing air molecules to create high-pitched frequencies

About the Author

Richard Fink IV is the creator of Throga, #1 Best-Selling Author in vocal education and labeled as the "world's leading online vocal coach" by the *Wall Street Journal*. Utilizing Skype since 2007, Richard has worked with clients in over 100 countries, spanning all 7 continents. He has taught Throga techniques to multi-platinum selling artists, TV and film actors, political leaders, Broadway stars, and singers signed to Warner Bros., Universal, Sony Music, Walt Disney, Columbia, Interscope, Atlantic, Mercury, and Broken Bow, as well as featured on Disney, Nickelodeon, The Voice (USA and Australia), America's Got Talent, The X Factor, American Idol, Yo Soy El Artista, Dancing with the Stars, and many others.

As a vocalist, Richard is a 3x Guinness World Record holder and award-winning singer for solo performances as Jesus (*Jesus Christ Superstar*) and Jean Valjean (*Les Miserables*). He released multiple albums as a songwriter and vocal-producer between 1991 and 2005, which led to co-writing and demoing songs for top charting artists such as Josh Groban and Michael Jackson.

Other career highlights as a vocal coach include touring with *Big Time Rush*, adjudicating the *Voice of DanceLife Unite* in Australia and the *Suncane Skale* competition in Europe, coaching at *Talent Camp at Universal Studios*, and speaking at JMC Academy (Berklee College of Music affiliate) in Sydney, Brisbane, and Melbourne. Most notably, Richard became the first person in history to be awarded a full-utility patent on a vocal training technique with the *7 Dimensions of Singing*.

www.ingramcontent.com/pod-product-compliance
Lightning Source LLC
Chambersburg PA
CBHW071426160426
43195CB00013B/1825